Hope for the Families

written by
ROBERT
PERSKE

illustrated by
MARTHA
PERSKE

Hope

New Directions for Parents of

ABINGDON PRESS

for the Families

Persons with Retardation or Other Disabilities

NASHVILLE

Library of Congress Cataloging in Publication Data

PERSKE, ROBERT.
  Hope for the families.
  1. Mental deficiency. 2. Mentally handicapped.
  3. Developmentally disabled. I. Perske, Martha.
  II. Title.
  RC570.P48   362.8'2   81-5700   AACR2

ISBN 0-687-17380-9

MANUFACTURED BY THE PARTHENON PRESS AT
NASHVILLE, TENNESSEE, UNITED STATES OF AMERICA

On July 2, 1972, six young men lost their lives while trying to save one another in the Missouri River. Five of those persons had retardation or other disabilities. One was their counselor. This book is dedicated to the memory of those six young men, and to their parents. . . .

Jesse Barber

John Hogan

Tom Madsen

Gary Olson

John Purnell

Ron Schultz

Contents

1. The Reason for This Book

This book is for families who are trying to turn a tough situation into a rich experience.

If you are the parent of a person with mental retardation, cerebral palsy, autism, epilepsy, a learning disability, or other developmental disabilities, or . . .

If you would like to be such a parent (many are becoming adoptive parents and agency-trained foster parents of persons with handicaps these days), or . . .

If you are the brother, sister, aunt, uncle, or grandparent in such a family, or . . .

If you are curious about what can go on in such families and in their surrounding neighborhoods . . .

This book is for you.

It contains a series of eye-opening, direction-giving signposts meant to guide the families of persons with handicaps out of the unfair, isolated, Dark-Age existence into which society once forced them. That Dark Age—believe it or not—never really began to fade away until just three decades ago. Before that time, the signposts would have pointed merely toward distant fog-shrouded areas where there were misty outlines of persons . . . or moving blurs . . . or nothing at all.

We, an author and an artist, stirred these fresh guideposts—these new ways of thinking about persons with handicaps—around in our minds and put them into brief, easier-to-understand art and print vignettes. At least we hope they are easier to understand . . . and we hope they will point the way toward better lives for families of persons with handicaps . . . and if they have better lives, we think the rest of civilization will be better off, too.

Robert and Martha Perske

PERSKE '80

So what did you expect? Superbaby? Of course you did. Every mom and dad dream that their forthcoming child will be a superbaby. Remember those secret thoughts? "Maybe our child will be . . .

a president
or a prime minister
a famous scientist
an all-star athlete
a celebrated musician
a 'mother-of-the-year'
a brilliant author
a sensitive artist
or a saint."

Whatever you fantasied about your unborn child probably had something to do with the person you wanted to be—but never could. And the closest you came to facing your secret expectations showed up in statements such as, "I only hope it's healthy."

Everybody quietly hopes for a superbaby, but nobody gets one.

Many times those who actually become great leaders, scientists, or artists do so out of a personal need to compensate for deficiencies and defects in their lives. And their success is often an utter surprise to their parents—mothers and fathers who felt that *this one* was too sickly, nervous, loud, or strange.

Consider These Options

● Accept the fact that the "child of your dreams" never was and never would have been. All parents must acknowledge this sooner or later. Your problem: You must do it sooner.

● Love your child exactly as he or she is. Real love does not demand that persons change into what we want them to become before we can start loving them.

● Take advantage of the early discovery of your child's handicap. The sooner you find professionals and advocates willing to help you and your youngster, the better. *Early intervention is crucial.*

● Take comfort in knowing it is better that your child's birth came now, rather than thirty years ago. Today, supportive persons are available in the community; there are even parents available who have experienced what you are going through. Their number grows each year. Thirty years ago, you would have been torn between two terrible choices—keeping your child at home with no help from anyone . . . or sending your youngster away.

So let the child of your mind die. Let the real child live!

You will have them, all right. You may wonder if you are losing your mind. Probably not. But strange times will come, and getting through them takes energy and grit.

Some experts have described in detail the stages you are expected to face. The only trouble is that parents who are adjusting to children with handicaps do not follow a set course. Each parent reacts differently.

Here are a few oversimplified descriptions of stages you may—or may not—experience. And many parents could add to this list.

The Drags. It is as if your spring had run down. You feel so tired you can hardly drag yourself around. The sun may be shining, but to you the day seems cloudy. You may feel a lump in your throat or knots in your stomach. It is hard to breath, and every once in a while you may hear yourself sighing. You may even wonder if you have the flu. When these times come, you wish you could find a warm cozy hole, crawl into it, and close a lid after you.

This may be your mind's way of telling you that "out there," there is too much to take. So you slow down, withdraw, move within yourself, interact less with the world around you, and take some time out. This is OK, providing you do not stay out too long.

The Speeds. When this stage approaches, you feel as though somebody has wound your spring too tightly. You move around at a frenzied pace . . .

so much to think about
so much to do
so much ground to cover
so many places to go
so many people to see.

It is as if a combination of the Ten Commandments and St. Vitus Dance energizes your movements. Many new ideas and concepts which need to be acted upon come to your mind. It is your personality's way to "get at it," even if some motions are wasted.

The Blocks. Tough news came from the doctors. But somehow your ears refused to hear what they told you, and your eyes remained blind to the evidence they presented. The knowledge that your child possesses a handicap is hard to take. You may even talk to others as if your child has no handicap. That is OK for awhile. Parents' minds need time to change from believing their child's a superbaby to seeing that child as he or she really is. It is all right to make this shift slowly. But it is unhealthy if it is never made.

The Hurts. No professional can describe all the types of anguish and pain parents feel after learning their child has a handicap. Nevertheless, all of them hurt; they hurt badly!

Such pain can force you to become edgy and nervous; to walk floors or lie awake all night, tossing and turning; or to break down and cry—fathers included.

Bear in mind that when you do feel such pain, it may be your body and mind saying to you that you are strong enough to bear the hurt you must feel. It is my hunch that you will never suffer pain beyond what you can endure. There are many mechanisms within you to dull the senses when things become overwhelming. Some people can become stronger from enduring pain.

If you happen to be hurting while reading these sentences, you may feel anger toward the author of these words. That is OK, too. This book is not intended to bring you comfort. Its purpose is to help you grow and adjust so that you can accept, love, and act creatively on behalf of your child. You cannot do this without experiencing some hurts, enduring them, and working your way through them.

The Guilts. At times you may feel you have committed some horrible sin against God and man. You may even look deeply into your past, searching for that single horrid act that caused it all. But I am willing to wager that no matter how hard you search, you probably will never find such a cause.

Nevertheless, on some days you feel sure that you must be the worst human specimen on the face of the earth. Somewhere, somehow, you committed an unpardonable sin, and now you are paying for it.

Such guilt is phony. It is not the same kind of guilt you feel when you are caught with your hand in the cookie jar—or when you commit other real transgressions of greater magnitude. Therefore, you need not drag out all the black things in your life, examining them one by one. This exercise only gets in the way of adjusting to your child's handicap.

The Greats. While a few days earlier you may have felt that you were the world's worst mom or dad, now it may come to you that you are one of the greatest. You secretly may feel that God has chosen you to bear this extra burden because you are more special than other human beings.

Of course, it is more pleasant to fantasize yourself as being great. It is better than feeling you are the world's worst. So enjoy it while you can. But be careful. Sooner or later somebody will say or do something to send you crashing off your pedestal. When that happens, it is to be hoped you will not fall into the guilt trap again. Instead, you may achieve a fresh stability from knowing you are not a superparent. But you aren't a superdemon either. You have your weaknesses and strengths, like everyone else.

The Hates. After hurting for a time, you may search irrationally for chances to blame others and hurt them. Almost anybody you can think of may become a target:
    your spouse
    your neighbor
    your doctor
    your minister
    your children
    your parents
    or in-laws.

So you watch and wait. Sooner or later, someone—being human—will say or do something to "justify" unleashing your anger at them.

Fortunately, your gracious friends and relatives often remain unruffled when you blow your stack at times like these.

It is all right to feel such anger and hatred, even though it is irrational. Acting on that anger, however, can be precarious. It could make others hurt . . . then you hurt because you caused them pain . . . and the vicious circle starts over again.

The Escapes. Sometimes when you awaken at 2:00 A.M., you may wish you could close your eyes and never open them again. These wishes usually will remain secret because you will be ashamed of them. Nevertheless, many parents of children with handicaps openly confess to going through stages when they felt such an urge to escape. In spite of such in-the-wee-hours-of-the-morning urges, grit your teeth and hang on. By the time the sun rises, the situation often looks brighter.

Consider These Options

● If you feel like ending it all . . . wait. In time you will realize that such escapes are stupid. They create more problems than they solve.

● Do not divorce your mate this week. Better to wait, even though you harbor fears that your spouse has rotten genes . . . or that it is all his or her fault. (Your marriage partner may be harboring secretly the same fears about you.) It is better to contain such fears for the present and try to work together as a team.

● Shout epithets if you must. But let it come as no surprise that your curses lack the power to shake the foundations of God, nor do they wither the earth. It may be wiser, however, to utter them under your breath, in order to save wear and tear on your throat.

● Do not blame your doctor. The news that your child has a handicap will hurt no matter how he or she breaks the news to you. On the other hand, if your physician, in relating to you and your child, develops irrational blocks, guilts, and greats because of the handicap . . . get yourself another doctor.

● If you find yourself in the drags, enjoy the misery only for a limited time. Then grit your teeth and get going. Move those muscles! Work! Scrub that sink or mow that lawn. Do it even though you do not want to.

● When the speeds come on, stop. Sit down for a moment. Then talk slowly, walk slowly. Pick only one of the 241,000 things you feel you should do that day, and do it.

● Learn to admit to yourself that no matter how real these feelings may seem, they are strange and irrational. They will pass.

● Know that time is your best friend. In time, beautiful sanity can grow out of the terrible chaos.

● Look around and choose genuine support-persons—key professionals, advocates, relatives, friends—who are capable of entering your struggle in a helpful way. More are available than ever before, so do not try to "go it alone." In an international symposium on persons with handicaps, the participants asserted that although the initial pain in parents (upon learning their child is handicapped) remains high, their ability to move through those bewildering stages became easier because of the outside support they received.[1] Also, in a report to the President it was learned that child abuse in one program was nonexistent because of the many helpful family supports from the outside.[2]

● Try to keep the "unbearables" you experience from overflowing onto your child with the handicap. After all, the barriers he or she must overcome or live with are almost unbearable, too. It does not help to heap more burdens on these children when it is all they can do to carry their own.

So, there will be bewildering times in your lives. But as you hang on and move through each one, you will find precious opportunities to be strong and tender at the same time—with yourself, with your child, and with those around you.

1. R. Perske, ed. *Improving the Quality of Life: A Symposium on Normalization and Integration: A Symposium of the International League of Societies for the Mentally Handicapped* (Arlington, Tex.: Association for Retarded Citizens, National Headquarters, 1977).
2. R. Perske, "A Coordinated Effort to Take the Risk Out of 'At Risk,' " *The Report to the President, Mental Retardation: The Leading Edge—Service Programs That Work* (Washington, D.C.: President's Committee on Mental Retardation, 1978).

Every child comes into a family somewhat like a rock thrown into a pond. The ripples caused by the new arrival affect everyone. Nobody in the family remains exactly the same. Everyone changes.

When a new youngster has a handicap, the family often expends energy beyond the ordinary. An increased sharpening of wits and widening of hearts become necessary so that the one with the handicap can be understood, loved, and accepted as a member of the close-knit family circle. On the other hand, some households become cold toward such a child, and those families change for the worse.

Healthy change involves two important activities. First, it involves the *giving up* of attitudes, pursuits, and friends.

Some parts of the family routine drop away.

Friends who cannot adjust to the situation make fewer visits.

Some job assignments become impossible to fulfill.

Certain cherished recreational outings are curtailed.

Memberships in some organizations lose their value.

Spending habits change.

World-views which do not make sense anymore collapse.

That is only a first meager list of losses experienced by family members when a child with a handicap comes into the home. No two lists are alike. Some losses cause great pain, while others do not.

Second, healthy change involves a *taking on* of fresh viewpoints, responsibilities, and relationships.

New chores come into the family routine—special appointments, conferences, transportation, and babysitting responsibilities serve as a few examples. (You will soon understand why some professionals believe the most important family-support service is *respite care!*)

Closer relationships with physicians, educators, and other professionals become necessary.

New knowledge about myriads of things having to do with handicaps must be acquired.

New friends with a deeper appreciation for persons with handicaps appear on the scene.

An alertness for legislation affecting persons with handicaps is sparked.

The completion of written applications and questionnaires for professionals and government agencies never stops.

Sometimes the new things you take on cause you anguish—but not always. At other times you experience exhilaration and excitement over the new things that are coming into your life. Healthy change is always a bittersweet process.

Face a hard fact: *All of life involves dying to some things and rising toward others.* Many might attribute the fact that their lives are satisfying and productive to the gracious way they let themselves die to some things and come alive to others. When something in life delivers a flattening blow, they possess the audacity and the resilience to get up and come even more alive than before.

The "coming alive" of many families of children with handicaps is beautiful to behold. They have expanded and enriched . . .
their knowledge
their tenderness
their faith
their ability to relate to others
their sense of social justice
their family interactions.

Somehow they found untapped energies they never knew they possessed, and they became people they never dreamed they could become. Mary McCurdy described the changes in her life as we sat in a Lincoln, Nebraska, restaurant in 1971.

Before Billie was born I was a different person. (Her son had Down's Syndrome.) I was active as an officer in Junior League. I was involved in bridge circles, and I regularly attended country club activities with my husband. I still go to the country club once in awhile. But something happened to me—to my image—so that Junior League and bridge did not mean as much. It's like some things had to die in me . . . some myths I believed about myself . . . some ways I saw myself. They had to die and I had to let them die. Now I'm glad. But at the time I fought against it.

That afternoon, I was in the audience while Mrs. McCurdy testified brilliantly for fifteen minutes at a senate hearing in the state capitol. With remarkable polish, she listed fourteen clear, succinct reasons for the funding of small, community-based, family-scale residences for adults with developmental disabilities. Mary was indeed a changed person.

Unfortunately, I also can share experiences in which parents placed children with retardation, cerebral palsy, or epilepsy at the institution where I worked, and then moved out of the state, leaving it up to us to trace them. Since many of those children deserved a brighter future than we could give them, and because of the downright lack of parental contact, the changes these parents made, in my opinion, were for the worse. But that was years ago, and such dumping of children—as if they were so much excess baggage—is on the decline.

Consider These Options

● When you feel the time is right, let each member of the family reminisce about the attitudes, activities, and friends they lost in the changing process. Then share the things gained.

● Think about the bewildering times you have moved through. Then reflect on the changes you experienced in your life because you faced them.

● Remember that the extra changes you achieved came from adjusting to two handicaps: (1) the real barriers in your child's handicap and (2) the irrational prejudices others harbor for persons with handicaps. When society grows up and the many unfounded myths and fears about handicaps diminish, the changes one undergoes will be closer to those involved in accepting a so-called normal child into the family.

● Change slowly. Be stubborn if you must and take your sweet time. Quick dramatic changes can be suspect. Those making them often find themselves on shaky ground and in danger of slipping back. Be content to move forward slowly and purposefully.

Change can be rough, but it can lead to an exciting future—better than you ever dreamed.

5. Changing World-views

Not so very long ago, you and I were conditioned to perceive persons with handicaps as deviants. They were seen as . . .

possessed by evil forces
carriers of bad blood
a drag on the community's resources
the products of illicit sex
subhuman organisms
too ugly to be seen in public
objects to be laughed at
a group that would outbreed us
people with contagious sicknesses
sexual monsters and perverts
children who never grew up.

Our parents and teachers conditioned us by what they said—or didn't say—to feel uncomfortable around those imperfect people. We were led to believe that if we got too close to them, something evil would rub off on us.

Consequently, persons with disabilities were condemned to struggle against *two* handicaps. One was the actual handicap. The other was the additional wounding they received from our prejudices.

Wasn't the handicap itself enough? Why did we have to cripple them further? Let me offer one theory to explain such behavior.

Once we believed fiercely that *the world was becoming better and better*. And in keeping with this belief, everyone was expected ultimately to develop . . .

a pure heart
a brilliant mind
a beautiful body
a successful marriage
a high-status job
and live in a perfect society.

Then along came a few defenseless persons with obvious physical and mental handicaps. Their presence rattled our plans for a perfect world as a high wind rattles a loose shutter. We didn't like that, and the result was that we could not stand to have them around us.

Then something happened. One country, in an effort to create a *superrace*, started a world war. By the time it ended, the minds of all humankind were trying to comprehend the terrible things some groups of human beings had done to other groups. All of us tried to understand what had happened in places like Buchenwald, Auschwitz, Hiroshima, Nagasaki, London, Bataan, Corregidor.

After World War II, our belief in the gospel of world perfection began to fall apart. And we were reminded of some terrible facts.

All of us have gaps in our bodies and minds.

All of us are unfinished.

Some of us can hide our deficiencies better than others.

None of us will ever achieve perfection.

Those of us who think we are closest to perfection may be most likely to drag the human race to new lows.

Today we do not know whether the world is getting better and better—we only know it is getting more complex.

And yet it is an astonishing fact that humankind's healthy interest in persons with disabilities began to mushroom after the Holocaust and the Atom Bomb. One cannot help wondering if there is a connection.

Consider These Options

● Become aware of the number of persons with handicaps in your neighborhood who are . . .

living in ordinary homes like yours
passing you on the streets

riding with you on public transportation
rubbing elbows with you in stores
going to school with you
working in the same building you do
sitting in the congregation of your church, synagogue, or mosque.

Try to imagine how many of these people would not have been present, or moving so freely in your neighborhood, thirty years or more ago.

● Without feeling you must prove that your world-view today is better than it was before your child with the handicap was born, make a comparison. Honestly try to evaluate the way you saw things then and the way you see them now.

6. Understandable Monkey Wrenches

Each of us came into this world as a small bundle containing thousands of developmental forces. Each tiny component, like a single musician in a gigantic symphony orchestra, played its part at precisely the right time. Altogether, those forces triggered an enlarging, strengthening, and deepening that enabled you and me to change from tiny babies into mature adults within approximately twenty-two years.

Most of us moved through this masterpiece of growth with comparative ease, but a small number did not. Somewhere, somehow, and usually with no warning, a few of us seemed to have a monkey wrench thrown into that developing system. A chromosome became broken or lost its way; an invading parasite interfered; a foreign substance upset the chemical balance; or a physical blow disturbed some of the workings. Of course, when this happened, many different people moved in as fast as they could to adjust the system and get it working again. But sadly, help for some of us did not get to the scene fast enough—or there was not yet enough knowledge and skill to repair the damage completely.

Afterward, development was never again as easy or as automatic for those of us who incurred such disabilities; it became like an obstacle course. And we were destined to work for the rest of our lives to overcome or to live with the wounds caused while we were growing up.

Over the years, I have watched hundreds of persons with developmental disabilities work like birds with short wings trying to keep up as well as they could with the others who grew and developed like soaring seagulls. After seeing how long and hard some of these people have struggled to achieve steps in their development . . . well, there is no dodging it—many have become heroes in my eyes.

Today, many persons with disabilities are being seen as heroes by their parents, too. The reason: Modern day professionals are able to show parents exactly what went wrong with their son or daughter's developing system. And these new-breed clinicians are getting better at their job each year.

Some years ago, when the "monkey wrenches" could not be pinpointed and understood, folks created myths to explain the cause of certain disabilities. Now such myths fade rapidly as the real explanations emerge, as you will see in these examples.

ITEM: A thoughtful psychologist showed the parents of seven-year-old Johnny Savin why he simply could not sit still and pay attention. The little fellow was literally a victim of his senses. While trying to listen to his mother or teacher, the noise of a truck outside, the ticking of a clock, a ray of sunshine coming into the window, the hum of a refrigerator motor—these things distracted him. They bombarded his sensory receivers, and unlike us, he was unable to focus on one item of sensory stimulation and tune out the rest. This knowledge enabled the parents and teachers to help Johnny attain fresh focusing and tracking skills. Some thirty years ago, his short attention span probably would have caused him to be seen as a wild, undisciplined child with "soft" parents . . . no matter how many beatings he received.

ITEM: The parents of seventeen-year-old Mary Manson know that the brain is a small dynamo that emits electrical charges—some on command and some not—which move all kinds of muscles in the body. They also know that periodically, large uncontrolled surges of electrons cause Mary to fall, suffer erratic muscle contractions, and remain unconscious for a time. They understand such epileptic seizures and they know what to do to keep such convulsions at a minimum. They have even trained Mary's boyfriend to help her handle seizures when they are alone . . .

to know when one is coming on

to keep her from hurting herself from a fall

to see that her tongue is not caught between her teeth

to position her head so she can breathe freely

to know that the convulsions cause her no pain (except for a slight muscle soreness afterward)

to help her rest a while after the seizure.

That seems simple enough. And yet, if Mary had lived in Salem, the Massachusetts Bay colony, in 1692, her convulsions would not have been taken so lightly. She would have been hanged as a witch!

ITEM: Harry Olson needs extra patience from his parents since his psychomotor system must work twenty times as hard as ours to move the muscles of his body. It means holding out a hand and waiting until Harry slowly and shakily moves until his hand can reach the outstretched one, clasp it, and shake it. This young man has a cerebral-palsy problem so severe he cannot speak. Nevertheless, Harry's parents and friends—through a series of questions and his nonverbal gestures as responses—taught him to play chess. Today he beats most of the people he plays! Harry also became an avid baseball fan, who one day proved that he had memorized the name and number of every New York Yankee ball player. Later he had enough sense to quit the Yanks when they started to lose. More recently, Harry uses a *communication board*—he speaks by pointing to words or spelling them out. He also types messages on a typewriter with a special keyboard. This all happened because Harry's parents were helped to understand the developmental barriers in his life. And yet I can remember working in an institution twenty years ago when people like Harry were diagnosed as *imbeciles*. They were allowed to fold up in a corner, doing nothing for days on end—many times sitting for hours in their own excrement.

ITEM: Mary Manero, age thirteen, an attractive girl with retardation and cerebral palsy,

labors constantly to swallow correctly. Saliva comes out of her mouth because the muscles of her throat fail to work properly. To counteract this problem, she moves her head and struggles as if she were attempting to swallow a golf ball. She carries tissues for wiping her mouth as much as she can, but still saliva escapes. Several years ago, the famous comic-strip character, Denny Dimwit, was drawn with droolings like Mary's falling from his mouth. If the artist had known what Mr. and Mrs. Manero know about this problem, he probably never would have created Denny Dimwit and made him such an object of ridicule. On second thought, maybe that artist did learn . . . and maybe that is why we do not see Denny Dimwit anymore.

ITEM: When Larry Ramirez was eight, he played strange games with himself. His hands and fingers moved in the same repetitive patterns for long periods of time—touching his right thumb with each of the four fingers . . . closing the hand into a fist . . . opening wide and then touching the thumb with each of the four fingers again. A physician and an educator helped Larry's parents to see that the environment outside this boy with autism was not as gratifying as the self-stimulating inner world he created for himself. But today at fifteen, Larry no longer carries out such repetitive rituals. Educators teamed with the parents to develop a detailed list of reinforcements (food, hugs, loving words, etc.) as rewards for interacting with people and things outside himself. It worked. The self-stimulating behaviors ceased. Nevertheless, in the first half of this century, thousands of people were placed in institutions because they performed bizarre-looking finger rituals, rocked, paced up and down in precise repetitive patterns, or banged their heads. And because people did not understand why they did it, and because they did not know how to stop them, those people fingered, rocked, paced, and banged, year after year in institutions, until they died.

ITEM: "I'm too dumb . . . I'm no good . . . I can't do it." Teen-ager Richard Bacall made statements such as these every time the going got rough, as a way to "get himself off the hook." Richard's parents let him get away with such behavior until a thoughtful counselor dared them to discover what their son could become if they did not let him give up so easily. Richard was helped to see good possibilities in himself and to accept the hardship and pain of striving to achieve what others saw in him. From that time on, that young man began to think of himself at times as a winner, not always as a loser.

ITEM: When ten-year-old Jimmy Yossarian moved with his family into a new neighborhood, he frequently would wander away and become lost. Jim's parents understood the orientation problems connected with his developmental disability, however, so almost every night that summer, Jim and his dad could be seen walking together in the new neighborhood. First, there were walks around the block. Then the walks encompassed other surrounding blocks. Later, they walked in definite directions away from their home. But these were more than walks. His dad continually talked to Jim about the things they saw and the places they passed. In a few months, Jimmy Yossarian walked his new neighborhood alone.

ITEM: Those of us who think we are smarties may pride ourselves on doing a good job of abstract thinking. We may become so good at it that we forget that good *concrete* thinking must come first. For this reason, your child with a handicap may thrive on simple concrete words. To such a person, "cookie" will mean something good to eat. If you tell that same person, "That's the way the cookie crumbles," do not be surprised if you are asked, "Where's the cookie?" A humorous example of concrete thinking happened years ago when Jimmy Phillipi, a nine-year-old with retardation, attended the funeral of an uncle. He didn't abstract everything that was going on; nevertheless, he was great at remembering the concrete details of what took place. Upon his return, he described a portion of the graveside service.

The men put my uncle who was in the box over the hole with straps across it. Then the minister stood at the end of the box. He raised his hand and said, "In the name of the Father and of the Son, and in the hole you go!"

Parents, being aware of this inability to understand certain abstract ideas, can experience the thrill of talking to their son or daughter on the child's own level.

ITEM: I have vivid recollections of big Joe Zarillo, a sixteen-year-old, whose way of showing that he liked me was to walk up and punch me in the stomach. This left me with two alternatives—to stay away from Joe and ignore him, or to face him and teach him better judgment. It wasn't easy—as I backed away—to say, "Look Joe, you're almost a man now and men don't hit each other in the stomach. They shake hands. . . . Now shake!" All of us must struggle to learn good judgment, and in some persons with disabilities this learning can be delayed. But to look away and ignore such childish actions may be one of the most hostile things we can do. All of us must work at improving our judgment as long as we live—and those with handicaps should not be exempted.

ITEM: I recall a little-league coach—who must have had a rather unsatisfactory athletic career himself—shouting at the top of his lungs to his right fielder on the move, "You drop that fly and I'll kill you!" When those threatening words struck the small boy's ears, fear grabbed him, and the ball struck the ground at his feet. Such blocking fears can be found in many people with developmental disabilities, but many mothers and fathers have become utterly brilliant in helping their children handle the blocks that keep those with handicaps from doing the best they can.

ITEM: The mother of three-year-old Patricia Kaprosky, a child with profound handicaps, began to feel that she was the worst mother in the world. During mealtimes, little Patty would stretch out like a board and scream as soon as a spoon touched her lips. Then Mrs.

Kaprosky—doing what good mothers do instinctively—would try to hold her daughter close and comfort her. But Patty would only shove her mother away. Finally, a visiting developmental therapist explained that such reactions did not constitute a lack of love for the mother, but were merely involuntary infantile reflex actions—such as all of us are born with—which had lingered, never having been replaced by normal voluntary actions. The therapist showed the mother how to "fold Patty like an accordian," bringing the child's knees up toward her chest and wrapping her little arms around her knees. In this position, Patty could relax her muscles, eat comfortably, and receive the warm hugging her mother wanted so much to give her. Today, many of Patty's infantile reflexes have faded. Her "bonding" to her mother has become cuddly, warm, and rich. Nevertheless, that mother had to understand a single functional quirk in her child and learn how to counteract it, before real love could flow between them.

One can see that this chapter could go on and on, describing the understandable monkey wrenches in the developing systems of persons with handicaps. Good! Until we began to pinpoint and describe these barriers to development, handicaps were explained away by terrible, unscientific myths. The victims were seen as inhuman, or as holy innocents, or as demon-possessed, or as sick. Some people were even convinced that developmental disabilities were caused by loose morals. I wish that the people who still believe those myths could see how hard some persons with retardation struggle to learn. They labor as one would suck a thick milkshake through a thin straw—they work so hard for what they get. And they *are* learning.

But until people understand the real barriers to development, you will have to put up with a lot of cockamamie explanations as to why your sons and daughters function as they do. Nevertheless, hang in there! The truth is on your side.

Consider These Options

● Develop an almost childlike questioning of the professionals. (Why does he do that? What causes him to do it? Can you explain it to me in words I can understand?) Do not stop asking until you understand the real barriers to the development of your son or daughter.

● Seize every opportunity to explain to relatives, friends, and neighbors, casually but clearly, your understanding of your child's barriers. Do not keep them in the dark.

● Urie Bronfenbrenner, the noted expert on human development, said, "Every child should spend a substantial amount of time with someone who's crazy about him . . . I mean there has to be at least one person who has an irrational involvement with that child, someone who thinks that kid is more important than other people's kids, someone who's in love with him and whom he loves in return."[1] When you replace the weird myths with real facts about your son or daughter, you may be in a great position to be crazy about your child.

● When you begin to see your child as a hero for working so hard to overcome the obstacles in his or her life, don't be modest! Share your views with everyone!

---

1. "Nobody Home: The Erosion of the American Family," *Psychology Today* (May 1977).

Not many years ago, we did not know very much about developmental disabilities, but we were brilliant in the way we labeled and classified people who had them. People were categorized by their disabilities . . .

quadriplegic
cerebral palsied
autistic
mentally retarded
learning disabled
epileptic
paraplegic
deaf-blind.

Some were labeled according to the way they looked . . .

mongoloid
gargoyle
hydrocephalic
cretin
microcephalic
dwarf.

Others were identified by the names of famous professionals . . .

Down's Syndrome
Prader-Willi Syndrome
Niemann-Pick's Disease
Von Recklinghausen's Disease.

These labels only scratch the surface—there are hundreds more.

When one speaks in that way about persons with handicaps, it is as if one has spied large, oversized badges pinned on them. The diagnostic words command such focused attention that one fails to see their other rich, attractive qualities. Such narrow vision can be cruel and unfair.

On the other hand, skilled professionals need diagnostic terms. Without them, efficient communication between colleagues about the many handicaps from which human beings suffer would be nonexistent.

The real tragedy is that these sophisticated labels created in clinics tend to trickle into the everyday conversation of ordinary citizens. Then they can become debilitating scare words. The day your friends are led to believe you are a paranoid, a schizophrenic, a retardate, a gargoyle, or a cretin, you can expect some of them to change their attitude toward you, even though they do not really know what the words mean.

Also, once you receive such a label, there will be a tendency to classify you as if you were an object, making it less possible for you to be seen as a valued, individual human being. Some will not see you as a person at all. Then comes the real danger. Since *nonpersons* are not expected to be capable of understanding, hurt, humor, or love, you may be heartlessly repulsed from the mainstream of community living, although with proper supports, your life in your own neighborhood could have been rich. It is not fair, but it happens.

Recently, it has been persons with handicaps themselves who are challenging us to look beyond the labels, to see them as they really are. In 1974, a group of former residents of the Fairview State Hospital and Training Center in Salem, Oregon, had been struggling to choose a name for their innovative new self-advocacy organization. During the debate, a young woman rose to speak. She said, "We are tired of being seen as retarded. We want to be seen as people, first!" The group, so touched by the woman's plea, dropped the other suggestions and named their organization People First! Today, People First organizations are springing up throughout Canada and the United States. And the descriptive title of that organization voices a deep longing of thousands of people down through the centuries who had wanted to be seen as people first . . . but nobody heard. Today, many of us do hear, and we do something about it.

Some new-breed professionals are trying. With a new sensitivity, they are doing everything they can to make sure that diagnostic labels do not belittle or demean those who receive them. They have developed a policy.

Use a label only as a noun referring to a condition (e.g., "a person with mental retardation").

Never use a label as a noun referring to a person (e.g., "the epileptic" or "the autistic").

Never use a label as an adjective (e.g., "the hydrocephalic person").[1]

Governments are beginning to look beyond labels, too. The United States government, in 1978, by Public Law 95-602, *abandoned the use of categorical labels in defining persons with developmental disabilities*. It focused instead on actual barriers that stand in the way of normal development. The law states that any person with substantial impairments in at least three of these seven functions of everyday living is in need of special understanding and help from the government:

1. self-care
2. receptive and expressing language
3. learning
4. mobility
5. self-direction
6. capacity for independent living
7. economic sufficiency.

But most remarkable of all, some ordinary citizens are picking up the knack of looking past the labels. One woman repeatedly holds dinner parties for the men and women with handicaps who live next door (she does it every time one of them achieves a new milestone in their development). She said, "It's fun having parties with these people. . . . People—I guess that's the key. I see them as people before anything else."

Imagine that. And she didn't even know about the famous plea of the woman from Salem.

Consider These Options

● Clean up your own language first. During the days that follow, you will interact with hundreds of people who will not be aware, as you are, of the latest word in addressing persons with handicaps. It is best not to try to clean up their language, as if multiple four-letter words have spewed from their mouths. Better to first practice using the new forms yourself. This task is not easy. You may have to catch yourself time and time again and go back and correct your own speech. It could take months to get it right. It did for me.

● Use the new forms of address in any articles or books you may be writing. It will give your editors nightmares, at first. But it is better that they have nightmares than to put one more into the lives of people having handicaps. I've battled three editors on this subject, and guess what? All three came around to my point of view.

● Consider a so-called category of labeled people—for instance, persons with Down's Syndrome. When several of them are together, notice how they function differently from one another—they are individuals. Then draw your own conclusions about the values and dangers of labeling and classifying people.

● See the suggested forms of address in this chapter as the latest word, if you like, but not as the last word. With the coming of every new day, your sons and daughters are being seen more and more as people, first—as valued, individual human beings. Within the next ten years, however, someone will come up with a better formula. Great! Let the day come soon.

---

1. The forms of address suggested by forward-thinking professionals and the plea of the woman from Salem have influenced me to construct the sentences of this book so that the words *persons, people, citizens,* and *human beings* appear first, and the words for their *handicapping condition,* second.

8. Theology: Bad to Better

On days when the problems of a handicap in your family overwhelm you, you may begin to think of God and of what the Almighty had to do with it all. Then the question, Why me, Lord? races through your brain . . . and sometimes slips past your lips as a soft, almost inaudible sigh. At other times the question comes out less softly!

Fortunately, you live in a time when you can take this burning question to sensible religious leaders, and more often than not, they will receive you with compassion and try to help you with your struggle. But it has not always been that way. In previous ages, your "why me" would have provoked some religious leaders to utter terrible judgments upon you.

Strange Switchings. In medieval Europe, some leaders would have tried to convince you that your child with the handicap was a *changeling.* Elves, trolls, fairies, or other so-called quasi-humans were thought to have removed the human infant from the cradle and replaced it with one of their own. With this belief, parents felt free to decide whether to keep their child, or reject it as not being human at all.

Strange Possessions. After two Dominican priests produced the world's most definitive handbook on identifying and trying witches (Jakob Sprenger and Heinrich Kramer, (*Malleus Maleficarum* [1846]), witch hunts became a frequent activity in many areas of Europe, and later in the thirteen colonies of New England. Looking back, these searches for the devil's cronies at work usually served as excellent outlets for the irrational fears some communities collected and stored because no other avenues for handling them existed. Unfortunately, such purgings did not go out of style in Salem until after nineteen panic-inspired hangings, two jailhouse deaths, and one pressing-to-death.

You could have accused your neighbor of being the devil's disciple and had him hanged because he made you sexually impotent, dried up your cow's milk, whirlwinded your barn, brought fevers to your family, caused your crops to fail or your lover to spurn you. However, that minority of persons with obvious handicaps in a community were especially scrutinized for evidence of evil possession. When ill-defined anxieties ran high in some locales, those with "fits," "hysterias," disfigured limbs, strange behaviors, and grotesque features died—or caused the death of someone else—because of their handicaps.

Although we smile a superior smile when we think about how silly people used to be, we must remember that our ancestors did not possess the down-to-earth explanations for such handicaps that we possess today. And because we still do not know everything about such situations, others in the distant future will smile a superior smile when they think about our response to persons with handicaps today.

Bad Matches. Not long ago, leading psychologists and sociologists viewed as scientific fact the theory that persons having "good blood" were virtuous and pure in heart, while the lineage of "bad blood" was laced with trollops; and anybody—especially females—who enjoyed an extravagant supply of sexual activity simply had to be feebleminded.

In 1912, this belief was amplified in a best-selling book by Henry Goddard, *The Kallikak Family* (New York: Macmillan & Co.). Goddard, a researcher, told the story of Martin Kallikak, Sr., a noble Revolutionary soldier of "good English blood of the middle class," who, at a tavern frequented by the militia during the war, met a "feeble-minded" unnamed woman. By this woman he became the father of a "feeble-minded" son. Later, the woman, in a not-so-feeble-minded way, named her son Martin Kallikak,

Jr. According to Goddard, Martin, Jr., then proceeded to bring into the world—with the help of his offspring during the next four generations—480 descendants, of whom 443 were judged to be feebleminded. In the meantime, Martin Kallikak, Sr., returned to his own high traditions of respectability. He married a woman "of his own quality" and four generations of their lineage produced 496 almost spotless and unblemished children.

Today, reputable scientists see the "scientific study" of the Kallikak family as downright spurious. Nevertheless, this book set off a *"eugenic scare"* which spread rapidly throughout the land. Leading scientists from prestigious universities organized the Eugenic Movement, which rallied behind a single goal—to encourage people with *good* blood to thrive and multiply; and to do everything possible to stop those with *bad* blood from unleashing a so-called raging river of fornication and procreation on the world, which would cause a horrendous degeneration of the human race.

Consequently, during the period from 1912 to 1936, feeblemindedness was right up there with venereal disease, suicide, and eternal damnation as clergy-molded punishments for messing around with loose women. The Kallikak story served as vivid illustrative material for many a minister's sermon. As a young boy, I recall an evangelist who introduced me to the debauching event and its terrifying results. His lurid descriptions made all the males in the congregation feel the need to increase distance between ourselves and all females—our fear-clouded minds making it impossible to tell which were "loose" and which were not.

This response was exactly what Goddard had wanted to provoke. Said he, "Now that the facts are known, let the lesson be learned; let the sermons be preached; let it be impressed upon our young men of good family that they dare not step aside for even a moment." Unfortunately, the sermon always was delivered at the expense of persons with developmental disabilities.

God's Special Children. In 1953, Dale Evans Rogers, the mother of an infant daughter with Down's Syndrome, wrote *Angel Unaware* (Los Angeles: Fleming H. Revell). In this book she described her daughter as a special emissary from God:

> I believe with all my heart that God sent her on a two-year mission to our household, to strengthen us spiritually and to draw us closer together in the knowledge and love and fellowship with God.
>
> It has been said that tragedy and sorrow never leave us where they find us. In this instance, both Roy and I are grateful to God for the privilege of learning some great lessons of truth through His tiny messenger, Robin Elisabeth Rogers.

Mrs. Rogers' book introduced a refreshing change in attitudes toward persons with developmental disabilities—a complete opposite to Goddard's belief. Instead of seeing them as products of sin, persons with handicaps were perceived as special angels. Ordinary citizens became more tolerant toward persons with handicaps and less prone to reject them as evil.

Others took the cue. A Roman Catholic order in San Francisco organized a program for persons with developmental disabilities and called it *The Holy Innocents.* Others began alluding to them as *God's children.* A remarkable improvement.

There were problems, however. These "holy innocents" grew up; they became bigger than some of us; they were able to push us around and do all kinds of unholy acts. It behooved us to recognize that we should begin to shape them as we do our other growing children.

What Is So Special? As long as we beheld them as God's special ones, persons with handicaps were set apart from us as if they were above humanity. Lately, however, we have come to see that they are more like us, than they are different from us. So why must there be an attempt to develop special theologies for persons with developmental problems?

We can honestly say this today, because most religions have given up any hope that their members will become perfect or near perfect. All humans are seen as persons, with limitations as well as strengths. Each of us struggles to make a good life out of our own uniqueness. All of us are limited to some degree. With this view of human nature, no one needs to be seen as less than human, or as more than human.

Back to the Big Question. And so anguished parents of persons with handicaps, down through the ages, have uttered a single painful question. Interestingly, parents received different answers at different times and places. And more interestingly, none of the answers out of the past will completely satisfy you, today's parents of those with handicaps, knowing what you know. So what is the answer for you? A parent, Ken Yockey, attacked the question in a playful but serious way when he wrote "Supplication."

AND THE PARENT OF THE MENTALLY RETARDED CHILD SAID HUMBLY: Why me Lord?

AND THE LORD SAID: But my son, why *not* you?

AND THE PARENT SAID: But Lord, what was my sin?

AND THE LORD SAID: My son, all men are sinners. You are not being singled out for punishment.

(Pause)

WITH TEARS STREAMING FROM HIS EYES, THE PARENT SAID: Then Lord, *why* me?

AND THE LORD SAID GENTLY: My son, be calm. I sense that you are becoming emotionally involved.

(Pause)

AND THE PARENT, BECOMING ANGRY, SAID: Dammit Lord, why *me?*

(Pause)

AND THE LORD'S VOICE RUMBLED FROM THE HEAVENS: My son, *now* I sense that you are becoming hostile.

(Long pause)

AND THE PARENT OF THE MENTALLY RETARDED CHILD SAID HUMBLY: Why me, Lord?

AND THE LORD SAID WITH A GREAT SIGH: My son, I shall reveal to you the truth. You and your wife were chosen because you have both the material and emotional means to raise and comfort such a child. You are both young, but you are both mature. You love each other and your other children, and you will love this child. You were chosen because you are among the best that *could* be chosen. My son, I have revealed to you the truth.

AND THE PARENT WITH GREAT HUMILITY AND AWE SAID: Thank you, Lord.

(Long pause)

AND THE PARENT SAID TENTATIVELY: Uh, Lord? Are you still there, Lord?

AND THE LORD SAID: Yes, my son.

AND THE PARENT SAID: Uh, Lord? Are you *sure* the Delivering Angel got the right address? Ours is 2200 Maple Street, the house on the corner: You know the one. It's the white house with a two-car garage, green shutters, hedges across the front of the lawn . . .[1]

Still no complete answer. Nevertheless, one interesting fact can now be known about this painful question. When times are tough and the going is hard—that is when we anguish. But when life is rich and everything is going our way, we forget all about the question, Why me?

Consider These Options

● Without tampering with the specifics of any one religion, you can believe that today your child with a handicap is seen as a human being, just as the rest of us are, subject to the same theological explanation of the nature of humankind that encompasses us all.

1. Ken Yockey, "Supplication," *We Have Been There*, ed. Terrell Dougan, Lyn Isbell, and Patricia Vyas (Salt Lake City, Utah: Dougan, Isbell & Vyas Associates, 1979).

● Now that many of the religious or quasireligious explanations that once belittled and dehumanized your child have crashed, three simple tenets may help make life with your child who has a handicap well worth living.

1. Believe that God is on the side of development in your son or daughter.
2. Believe that God is on the side of joy and that it was intended that you and your child achieve it.
3. Believe with all your heart that God has a rich sense of humor. Seeing the humor in a situation often makes it seem less grim. And if ever the day comes when we discover that God does not have a sense of humor . . . we are all lost!

After reading the previous chapter, you can see why the so-called scientific study of the Kallikaks and others like it (e.g., the studies of the Jukes, the Hill Folk, the Nams, and the Zeros) led to another terrible belief: *If we don't stop them, they will outbreed us.*

After knowing your own child, and others with handicaps in your community, you may find it hard to understand how Goddard and his colleagues came to that conclusion.

It may be even harder for you to believe that once in this century, prestigious scientists developed tests and definitions which led to the claim that more than half the citizens of North America were feebleminded. Following the publication of the *Kallikak Family,* some interesting events supported this belief.

In 1912, Goddard contracted with the United States Public Health Service to administer intelligence tests to newly arrived immigrants at Ellis Island. In his report, issued in 1913, he claimed that almost all persons born east of Germany were subnormal. According to his report, 80 percent of the Hungarians, 79 percent of the Italians, 87 percent of the Russians, and more than 90 percent of the Poles were feebleminded. On the other hand, Goddard claimed that the most intelligent immigrants were (in the following order): English, Dutch, Danish, Scotch, German, and Swedish.[1]

In 1917 and 1918, Robert Yerkes of Harvard supervised the mass intelligence testing of two million draftees for World War I.[2] From his test results, he claimed that more than half the United States troops were subnormal. Fortunately, his results were not published until 1921. By then the war was over, and we learned too late that most of our soldiers purportedly were not fit to fight.

In 1922, Lothrop Stoddard, in *Revolt Against Civilization* (New York: Macmillan Co.) claimed that the average mental age of Americans was equal to the fourteen-year-old mind. Interestingly, columnist Walter Lippman was one of the few persons who dared to speak out against this prestigious scientist. That year, writing in *The New Republic,* he stated that such a conclusion "is as precisely silly as if he had written that the average mile was three-quarters of a mile long."[3]

Unfortunately, in 1924, the United States Congress set up "national origin quotas" which favored western Europeans. These quotas were heavily influenced by the aforementioned scientists and their colleagues who had instigated the eugenic scare.

From 1924 until well into the 1940s, immigrants arriving at Ellis Island waited in long lines to face instant diagnosticians who looked closely, asked a few crisp questions, and occasionally chalked a cross with a circle around it on the back of some frightened foreigner. This dreaded mark meant that the person was judged to be feebleminded and was denied entrance into the United States.

At the same time such testing and culling was taking place on the borders of the continent, similar tests were administered to many citizens within the country. Such

1. Leon J. Kamin, "Heredity, Politics and Psychology," *The I. Q. Controversy,* ed. N. J. Block and Gerald Dworkin (New York: Pantheon Books, Random House, 1976).
2. R. M. Yerkes, *Psychological Examining in the United States Army,* vol. 15 (Washington, D.C.: Memoirs of National Academy of Sciences, 1921).
3. Walter Lippman, "The Mental Ages of Americans," *The I.Q. Controversy,* ed. Block and Dworkin.

testing usually took place after some crucial happening caused judges, educators, and physicians to pay special attention to them. Thousands who had been judged to be feebleminded packed the institutions of our land to overflowing.

And so, during the first forty years of the twentieth century, a fear lurked throughout the land that people with developmental problems comprised an astoundingly large army and would ultimately overpower us. Nevertheless, each time modern science managed to crate a breakthrough—to describe a particular disability in rational, easy-to-understand terms—myths fell away, and the estimated count of persons with handicaps became smaller. In 1977, the number of *all* persons with developmental disabilities was estimated by a task force of the United States government as being only 1.4 percent of the population.[4] The once-perceived overwhelming horde is really a tiny group of people.

You, the families of these persons, may experience a beautiful irony in your lifetime: Ordinary citizens are beginning to see your sons and daughters as they really are . . . to look past their disabilities and find attractive qualities . . . to respect them for the heroic efforts they exert in developing . . . to understand them and want them as close friends. As this happens, ordinary citizens will discover sadly that there are not enough persons with disabilities to go around. The demand will be greater than the supply. Some citizens will have to do without.

Consider These Options

• Although the myths created by Goddard and others in the early 1900s have died, you will discover that the ghost of Martin Kallikak, Sr., still rises up every now and then. For example, he may show up in the irrational fears of people who oppose the opening of a small, family-scale community residence for persons with special developmental needs. Such Kallikak-infected people usually are few, but can they ever be loud! *They* can sound like an overwhelming army! Perhaps you can share with such people some of the bits of information offered here. Do it carefully, however. After all, when there is a severe Kallikak scare, people become extremely emotional and their ear holes close up when clarifying facts are offered.

• Read Henry Goddard's *Kallikak Family*. Although it is out of print, most city libraries have copies. It can be read in less than an hour. Believe me—you won't believe your eyes!

• Conduct your own neighborhood survey. Delineate a certain area around your home. Develop your own method for finding out how many persons with developmental disabilities live within the area you have outlined. Also, find out how many so-called normal people live in that area. Then compute the percentage. The results could be interesting.

---

4. The National Task Force on the Definition of Developmental Disabilities (HEW's Developmental Disabilities Office) made the following estimates: mental retardation .5%, cerebral palsy .3%, epilepsy .25%, autism .05%, learning disability .1%, all other developmental disabilities .2%.

10. The Developmental Principle

In January, 1977, in Madison, Wisconsin, principal Jerry Johnson and a group of his Glendale Elementary School parents and teachers visited Badger School, an independent special school for children with severe and profound handicaps. Tentative plans called for closing Badger and transferring thirty-two students to Glendale. Therefore, it made sense to look in on the new Glendale candidates. The visitors looked . . . and they left in shock. Never before had the visitors seen so many children with wheelchairs, braces, positioning chairs, and disfigured limbs—disabilities compounded by severe learning, eating, and toilet problems. "I drove some of the parents and teachers back to Glendale in my car," said principal Johnson, "and everybody sat speechless. Finally, one of them blurted out what everybody was thinking: 'Do you mean we are going to mainstream those kids?' "

In September of that year, after seven months of cooperative interactions among the students, parents, and faculties of both schools, the thirty-two students were transferred to Glendale without a hitch. The exodus proved so remarkable that the sequential steps involved in the merger were recorded in a report to the president of the United States (Perske, *Mental Retardation: The Leading Edge*).

What caused the change in attitude? Pat Van Deventer, the director of educational programs for the thirty-two, put her finger on it.

> We did everything we could to help people see measurable development in our children. We showed video tapes of our children before they began a training sequence; then we showed video presentations of the same children taken months later. People saw with their own eyes how much each child achieved in school. That's what did it. Once they found our kids were developing, too, they spoke kindly about their moving to Glendale. They said things like 'I think our kids will learn more from your kids than yours will learn from ours.' "

The developmental principle has illuminated dark, shadowy beliefs like a bright beam of light. It helps us to see that just as you and I have our own rates of growth that are different from those of everybody else, so does your child with the handicap. The highest dignity and greatest joy in living comes not from trying to be what others are, but from developing into the best persons we can be, with the unique strengths and weaknesses we possess.

Although each of us shapes up differently, all of us are still developing. This can be seen when someone tells us that we cannot do a certain task. That usually makes us work harder to prove that we *can* do what our detractor says we cannot. Sometimes—to our surprise—we are successful. And when that happens, we feel simply great; at other times, however, we fail. Nevertheless, *we had the chance to try.*

Until recently, persons with developmental disabilities were not given the same chances to develop that we are given. The professionals in charge of their care predicted what they could or could not learn. For example, I recall institutions years ago where persons with Down's Syndrome were seen as "no-program kids" who could learn nothing; most of them were expected to die before they reached their teens. With pain, I also can recall persons with cerebral palsy who undoubtedly possessed normal or above intelligence, but who lived and died without our ever discovering their intellectual strengths. Because they could not move the muscles of their mouths well enough to speak or control the movements of their limbs well enough to gesture, we assumed their development was frozen. Of course there was no malicious intent; many professionals of earlier days simply did not know any better.

This is another reason your child is lucky to be born at this time in history. The imposing of *our* limits on the development of persons with handicaps is diminishing. We have discovered that all children—regardless of their handicaps—have their own inimitable milestones of growth which can unfold before our eyes if we let them. All we have to do is *recognize* the unfolding strengths and skills, know how to *cue* for them and draw them out, and *reinforce* them when they emerge.

Seeing your child develop according to his or her own rate of growth can be good for you, too. It can have a liberating effect. You can learn that "my child is not me" and that there is no hell-bent need to make your child a reasonable facsimile of yourself. Then you will be more free to help your child develop into the person he or she really can be . . . and you may enjoy watching it happen!

Consider These Options

● Ponder the notion that you have an excellent opportunity to be one of the most brilliant developmentalists your child will ever know.

● More professionals than ever before are available to help you learn how to *pinpoint* your child's next developmental step, to *cue* for it, and to *reinforce* the skill when it is achieved. Choose professionals from the many with whom you seem to click and persuade them to teach you what they know.

● Learn all you can about *individual program plans*. Know that a plan you can understand is the plan that will help your child most.

● Relax in the knowledge that you do not have to sweat and fret from now until 2:00 A.M. tomorrow morning about the next fifty-three steps your child must take in his or her developmental climb. Concern over the next single step is quite enough.

The developmental model can become contagious. Once those unrealistic expectations you harbored for your son or daughter no longer cloud your vision, you may reach an interesting new conclusion. Small realistic gains can become golden moments when they appear at your house. I will explain.

When children learn to sit up in their cribs, they can raise their intellectual functioning and adaptation at a tremendous rate. Looking at the ceiling is not half as stimulating as watching people and trying to understand what is going on.

When children can crawl, they can move about in their world and explore much more. They feel and touch more things. Moving targets and objects that make sounds call for apprehension and investigation. Such maneuverings increase their understanding and adaptation significantly.

When children learn to walk (or propel themselves in wheel chairs)—Bingo! They can really move about in their world.

When they learn to run or move fast, it is even better (although there will be times when you will doubt this).

When they become toilet-trained, they have gained a monumental milestone in our society. Now they can travel with you all the way around the world. Earlier, they probably would have been left at home because of their diaper-bound condition and their proneness to "accidents."

When they learn to come in out of the rain and generally to protect themselves from other elements in the environment, they can be trusted to carry out specific errands. This makes them proud.

If they can talk and ask for things, offer things, or express themselves—both likes and dislikes—they reach the high status of being a verbal communicator!

In normal children, all these achievements are taken for granted. But not if your child has a handicap. Then each gain is important. It amounts to a part of what can be called *survival learning*.

Parents are not the only people who can help a child with a handicap reach each achievement. Brothers, sisters, grandparents, aunts, uncles, and neighbors have been known to join in the pinpointing, cuing, and reinforcing of these small but golden gains. And each new milestone reached becomes a cause for celebration. I know family teams who have come together for a joyous occasion because a person learned to . . .

suck from a straw
control tongue movements
roll over
crawl
hold a spoon
get dressed
recognize safety signs
count money
shop alone
ride a bus alone
worship in a church, synagogue, or
   mosque
use proper manners
sit with a friend who is ill
get a job and hold it
live alone in an apartment.

Since so-called normal children grow by leaps and bounds, achievements like these are taken for granted. Not so for a child with a handicap. Every minimal gain can be monumental.

Consider These Options

● Remember when Tom Sawyer's friends were watching him whitewash the fence? They became interested, and before long, they were eager to join him in the task. You might casually let others know what pinpointed skill you are helping your child learn. Then see how many other family members and neighbors become interested in helping. Of course, everybody will not be takers. But you may be surprised by how many will.

● Become trigger-happy about celebrations. On days when your child "makes it" and does something better than he or she ever did before, call others in . . . and throw a party!

12. Human Dignity

For more years than we care to remember—before 1940—parents of children with handicaps often suffered miserable, lonely existences. Fellow citizens often treated such families as if they harbored a "Jonah" who needed to be thrown overboard.

Some physicians and dentists refused to treat these children.

Public schools closed their doors on them (even though they paid school taxes like everyone else).

Police automatically placed some persons with disabilities on suspect lists for unsolved neighborhood crimes.

Other parents ordered their children to stay away from those with developmental problems.

When some came into contact anyway, a few mothers saw to it that their children washed their hands afterward.

Community agencies offered no services and gave no support.

Clergy probed for sins the parents of these "odd ones" may have committed.

There were terrible family pressures. Many parents were made to feel that their sons and daughters should be treated like Hansels and Gretels—that they should be taken off and left somewhere.

Of course, parents resisted such pressures until they could go it alone no longer. Then they did the only thing left to do: They placed their children with handicaps in institutions.

I recall facing such mothers and fathers who applied for admission at institutions. Vivid recollections remain of one superintendent who gave the same speech to each set of parents. Only the names were changed: "Mr. and Mrs. Jones, Johnny is in our family now. All you need to do is forget this situation and go on making a life for yourselves and the rest of the family. Johnny is in our hands now."

Then the parents drove away from the institution without their child.

For many parents, however, the problem was not solved—they were not good forgetters. They continued to anguish over their children in institutions. And they felt utterly powerless.

It was this painful powerlessness that motivated some parents to look for others who were suffering the same plight. And when they got together, they shared in one another's sufferings. But they did not stop there. They organized their sharing sessions and held regular meetings . . . a few professionals joined as helpers . . . they developed a together-we-can-do-things-that-none-of-us-can-do-alone attitude.

By 1955, all kinds of voluntary associations for persons with developmental disabilities had set up national organizations throughout the United States and Canada. Then the first product of their organizing became apparent: They formed a respectful backlash—a counter force—aimed at all those who belittled and demeaned their children. They literally began talking back to physicians, educators, police, clergy, politicians, neighbors, and society in general.

While they organized, many of us who were working in institutions observed their activities from a distance. We "analyzed" them and shook our heads; we concluded that they were overly upset parents who, out of guilt, were going too far. After all, we believed, they would never be able to help themselves. Only *we* could help them.

Then, in the early 1960s, David Vail introduced the *principle of human dignity*, and it gave wings to the parents' organized backlashes.

It began when Vail, the medical director of Minnesota's Department of Public Welfare, held special workshops in all kinds of institutions throughout the state. He enabled inmates and staff alike to identify the many things that belittled residents of institutions, forcing them to function as less human. At climactic points in each workshop, he asked the participants to describe the things that dehumanized them. Here are a few responses taken from a longer list.

Dehumanization is . . .
having everything taken away upon arrival (such as a ring with sentiment)
lining up before the office door, one each hour, for a cigarette
being brought to the hospital handcuffed to a sheriff or a policeman
toeing the line for someone's convenience
having a haircut like the rest of the bunch
earning a dollar for eight hours of hard labor
having your hair curled when you'd rather wear it straight
not being able to go trick-or-treating on Halloween
not having becoming clothes to wear
not having a pet to care for
not having the privilege of decorating one's room
having your mail opened and censored so that the employees know Uncle John has had a gallbladder attack or Aunt Harriet is still on the relief roles
tailoring clothes with safety pins
being transferred to another institution without knowing why, where, or when.

But David Vail also helped people contribute to another list.

Human dignity is . . .
selecting one's own clothing and accessories

being able to get a cool drink without having to ask for it
having your own dresser, or even one drawer, for your own personal belongings
being able to evaluate your appearance in a full-length mirror
being called Mrs., Miss, or Mr.
being able to go to meals by yourself and not at an exact set time
having becoming clothes to wear
having a pet to care for
having a penny in the pocket
being treated like a patient when you are ill, not as if you were being punished
being provided with as much freedom and decision making in daily activities as your condition allows
having love
having self-respect and pride
being allowed to be yourself
being appreciated for what you are worth
being respected as a human being
having funds to pay for eyeglass repair and false teeth.

Vail organized these lists and published them in *Dehumanization and the Institutional Career* (Springfield, Ill.: Charles C. Thomas, 1964), a book aimed at changing the attitudes of professionals in institutions. Sadly, most professionals never learned about the book. But parents in voluntary organizations did. Then with an uncanny skill, they created their own "dehumanization versus dignity" lists. Such lists continue to be upgraded, even today.

Consider These Options

● Here is an exercise you and your family can have some fun with. Either separately or together, make two lists.

1. Make a list of all the things you could do that would belittle and dehumanize your child in your own home. Of course, this is not a list of things you actually have done—only things you know could be done.
2. Make a list of all the things you could do that would give your child a greater sense of human dignity and value in your own home. Focus on every little thing you can think of. Those little things can add up . . . and lead to a more dignified life for everyone.

Since the mid-1940s, the families of persons with handicaps throughout Canada and the United States have multiplied their successes. From the many breakthroughs, let me share a few that stand out in my mind. Families of persons with all kinds of developmental disabilities, on or about . . .

1947—began getting together and sharing in one another's struggles

1952—started their own voluntary associations

1958—became a positive force for changing public attitudes toward persons with handicaps

1963—martialed their forces behind the *principle of human dignity*

1964—energetically emphasized the *developmental principle.*

With each achievement came the increased sensitivity and vision needed for discovering the next. There was no stopping them! They no longer believed they were traumatized parents, helpless victims who could do nothing about their situation. Then they discovered the *principle of normalization.*

Although the normalization idea did not become embedded in the thinking of North Americans until the late 1960s, it was born ten years earlier in Scandinavia. The first notion was probably conceived by N. E. Bank-Mikkelsen, the director of the Danish Mental Retardation Service. According to information gained from Bank-Mikkelsen during a visit to California some years ago, he began to compare his own life with the lives of residents in institutions. "He thought of comforts he enjoyed, sofas and stuffed chairs, spacious and colorful rooms, a private bedroom and bath. He thought of his stylish clothes and his television set. He could find no justifiable reason for the disparity, and he began to search for a better alternative." As a result, he developed the "concept of normalized settings," which he described as "letting the mentally retarded obtain an existence as close to the normal as possible."[1]

Other Scandinavian countries picked up on this bold idea and two Swedish leaders, Karl Grunewald and Bengt Nirje, came up with a refined definition: "Making available to all mentally retarded people patterns of life and conditions of everyday living which are as close as possible to the regular circumstances and ways of life of their society."[2]

It was Gunnar and Rosemary Dybwad, leaders in the voluntary parent movement in North America, who began calling our attention to the principle of normalization as they lectured and consulted throughout the United States and Canada.

Then another American, working closely with the voluntary movement in Nebraska, proposed a technical definition: "Utilization of means which are as culturally normative as possible, in order to establish and/or maintain personal behaviors and characteristics which are as culturally normative as possible."[3]

Later, it was Nirje, the leader of the Swedish parent movement, who put the principle into its most poetic form.

Normalizaton means . . . a *normal rhythm of the day.*
You get out of bed in the morning, even if you are profoundly retarded and physically handicapped;
you get dressed,
and leave the house for school or work, you don't stay home;
in the morning you anticipate events,
in the evening you think back on what you have accomplished;

1. California Health and Welfare Agency, *Way to Go* (Baltimore, Md.: University Park Press, 1978).
2. R. Kugel and W. Wolfensberger, *Changing Patterns in Residential Services for the Mentally Retarded* (Washington, D.C.: President's Committee on Mental Retardation, 1969).
3. W. Wolfensberger; B. Nirje; S. Olshansky; R. Perske; and P. Roos, *The Principle of Normalization in Human Services* (Toronto: National Institute on Mental Retardation, 1972).

the day is not a monotonous 24 hours with every minute endless.

You eat at normal times of the day and in a normal fashion;

not just with a spoon, unless you are an infant;

not in bed, but at a table;

not early in the afternoon for the convenience of the staff.

Normalization means . . . *a normal rhythm of the week.*

You live in one place,

go to work in another,

and participate in leisure activities in yet another.

You anticipate leisure activities on weekends,

and look forward to getting back to school or work on Monday.

Normalization means . . . *a normal rhythm of the year.*

A vacation to break the routines of the year.

Seasonal changes bring with them a variety of types of food, work, cultural events, sports, leisure activities.

Just think . . . we thrive on these seasonal changes.

Normalization means . . . *normal developmental experiences of the life cycle.*

In childhood, children, but not adults, go to summer camps.

In adolescence, one is interested in grooming, hairstyles, music, boyfriends and girlfriends.

In adulthood, life is filled with work and responsibilities.

In old age, one has memories to look back on, and can enjoy the wisdom of experience.

Normalization means . . . *having a range of choices, wishes, desires respected and considered.*

Adults have the freedom to decide,

where they would like to live,

what kind of job they would like to have and can best perform.

Whether they would prefer to go bowling with a group, instead of staying home to watch television.

Normalization means . . . *living in a world made of two sexes.*

Children and adults both develop relationships with members of the opposite sex.

Teenagers become interested in having boyfriends and girlfriends.

And adults may fall in love, and decide to marry.

Normalization means . . . *the right to normal economic standards.*

All of us have basic financial privileges and responsibilities, are able to take advantage of compensatory economic security means, such as child allowances, old age pensions, and minimum wage regulations.

We should have money to decide how to spend, on personal luxuries or necessities.

Normalization means . . . *living in normal housing in a normal neighborhood.*

Not in a large facility with 20, 50, or 100 other people because you are retarded.

And not isolated from the rest of the community.

Normal locations and normal size homes will give residents better opportunities for successful integration with their communities.[4]

The principle of normalization has become a remarkable enlightener for the families of persons with handicaps. It has illuminated hundreds of nooks and crannies in the field of developmental disabilities that heretofore had been dark and shady. Parents used the principle to cast fresh light on their own dealings with their sons and daughters with handicaps. It also provided a common language with human-service professionals. As a result, the quality of living for persons with handicaps began to rise more sharply after 1967 than ever before in history.

Although the principle is extremely positive, its strongest function lies in its power to uncover conditions and practices which for centuries had *denormalized* people with handicaps, and to which little attention had been paid. If you lived in the institutions I knew in the late 1960's, here are some grim situations the principle would have exposed. You would have been found . . .

4. Canadian Association for the Mentally Retarded, *Orientation Manual on Mental Retardation* (Toronto: National Institute on Mental Retardation, 1977).

getting up at 5 A.M. and being dressed and fed before the 7 A.M. change of shift

going to bed early for the convenience of the staff

being seen as one of a group—seldom as an individual

eating, sleeping, recreating, and working within the same walled-in area

wearing "community" clothing

spending mealtimes in large, noisy, odoriferous dining rooms or being fed while lying on your back in bed

being forced to eat rapidly in order to adhere to a group schedule

never being in a room by yourself

always feeling you were a few notches below the staff and wishing you were as good or as privileged as they

working in the laundry for a dollar a week

receiving payment in coupons because you were not trusted with money

being told by the chaplain that if you minded the aides and worked hard, you would get out some day

knowing that most professionals kept looking for your sicknesses and your weaknesses, instead of your strengths

seldom being allowed to decide anything for yourself

suffering the low expectations of those around you when you tried anything new

seldom or never interacting with persons in regular communities

existing in a setting apart from those of the opposite sex

never riding in a staff person's private car because of institutional rules

sitting for long hours in "day rooms," with no programs

traveling in buses with the institution's name on the sides

being expected to die young

and then being buried in the institution's cemetery with your "patient number," instead of your name, on the tombstone.

Until the principle of normalized settings arrived on the scene, those of us who worked with persons having developmental disabilities often did not know any better than to treat them as we did. But we sometimes shudder when we think of the past. And we are happy to leave it all behind, as something historians will ponder at some future date.

A warning, however. Never does the principle argue for the normalization of people. We never would agree upon what is "normal." Instead, it calls for normalized environments, which are more nurturing to persons with handicaps than the artificial, out-of-the-way environments in which they used to live.

Just think . . . twenty years ago, who of us even would have dreamed that enabling persons with handicaps to live in a relatively normal setting would become an accepted way of life.

Consider These Options

● Give your child every chance to live in as normal a setting as possible.

● Do the same for yourself.

● Sometimes the two settings will clash. That is OK. Take your time; ponder the conflict; then make your choices. Both of you can be stronger from such decision making.

● At other times, your normalized environment and that of your child will be the same.

● Keep a good balance. Build the best nest you can for your child, but build the nest for yourself as well.

---

14. Risk, Courage, and Heroism

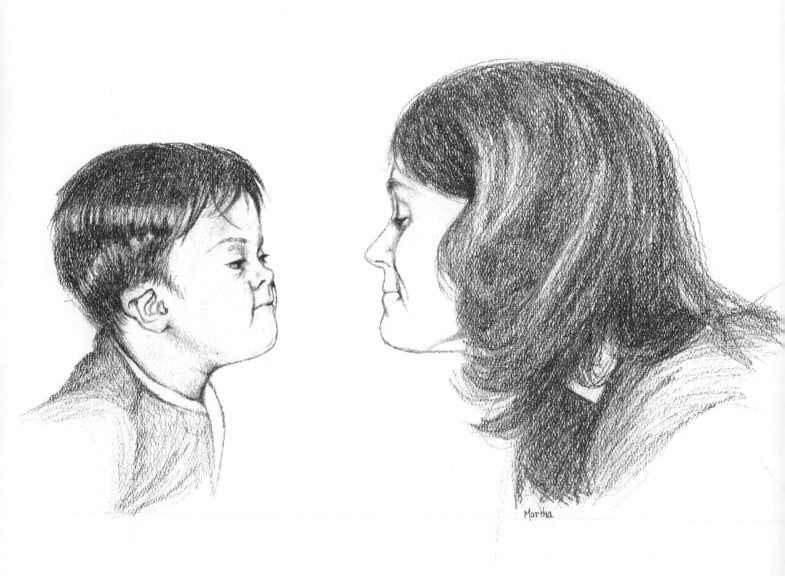

When we read about poor Tiny Tim in Dickens' *Christmas Carol*, something within us says, "Protect him . . . keep him safe . . . take care of him . . . make him comfortable." Even after his presence in the story helps to change the life of Ebenezer Scrooge, Tiny Tim Cratchit *remains unchanged*. We continue to see him as the same helpless little pity who needs special protection, safety, care, and comfort. It never occurs to us that the young man might become fed up with such smothering and tell us all to go #@*#@!

If someone tried to smother us with such excessive protection, we would assert ourselves quickly; we would announce our intentions to live our own lives, thank you, and make our own decisions. And if others refused us this freedom, we would tell them to back off in no uncertain terms. But until recently, persons with developmental disabilities were automatically subjected to an overprotected environment. Times are changing.

ITEM: "Of Human Courage and Dignity" was the title of an article by Wolf Wolfensberger that appeared in an August, 1970, *Omaha World Herald*. He told about the courageous actions of a young man with Down's Syndrome.

> The director of a local sheltered workshop had just received a letter from a mother whose two sons had perished in a fire which had destroyed their home. One of the sons, already a young adult, had been a worker in the workshop because he had Down's Syndrome and was severely retarded. The letter, with spelling errors and exactly as written, follows:

> Dear Mike & all
> I was in North Platte on a monday but the shop was close. I wanted to thank all of you for every thing you had done for Robert. He was so proud of his job and the ability to do things on his own.
> I am very proud of him as he went to the back room to save his brother. He had Donald from the head of the bed to the foot if he had only a few more minutes he would of had Donald out—even tho we know Donald was dead at the time.
> I am sending his one check back as they say it would not go through the machine. put the money in your fund so your books will balance.
> To day was my first day back at work. It was a long day but I know I have to keep busy. My two boys was my whole life so now I have to start over. My husband is very under standing—was hurt very bad also.
> If I can be of any help at any time please feel free to let me know. I feel I proved to the world a retarded child has a place in the world and can be a use ful person.
> Many thanks for every thing.
>   as ever
>   (Signature and town of residence)

> The check the mother enclosed . . . was burned at the edges.

ITEM: Some years ago a ten-year-old boy with severe retardation wandered away from a Midwest institution and became lost in the woods skirting the facility. The temperature was below freezing, and all off-duty personnel were called in to form emergency search parties. Two teen-agers with retardation, Ray and Elmer, asked me, a staff member, if they could search for the boy, too. I "moved through channels" and, after some time, received approval for the boys to join in the search. They found the lost boy! Later, the superintendent gave Ray and Elmer letters of commendation at a special ceremony. By that time, many of us at the institution were haunted by the fact that there were many teen-agers living there who functioned every bit as well as Elmer and Ray. Our obsession with being good protectors of the residents had blinded us to their value in such an emergency—they could have been mobilized much more efficiently and quickly than the off-duty staff.

ITEM: In *Das Schloss Der Barmherzigkeit* (Stuttgart: Quell-Verlag, 1960), Wilhelm Tuefel describes the response of children and adults with developmental disabilities, in an institution at Stetten, Germany, when the Nazi Party began their euthanasia program. In 1940, two gray buses with painted-over windows arrived periodically. Each time, the buses were loaded with residents who were "transferred" to a crematorium in a castle called Grafeneck, some miles away. It did not take the residents long to sense what was taking place. Then some amazing acts of courage began to happen. Many who could walk became deeply concerned for the nonambulatory persons, knowing they could not fend for themselves. Many moved to well-planned hiding places every time they saw the buses coming up the road. Said one boy after the buses left, "They didn't catch me. I'm smarter than they." Karl, a teen-ager, fought with the driver and ran away shouting, "I'll hang myself before I'll die like that." Richard, with spastic legs, knew he did not have a chance. He calmly gave his pocket money and watch to his closest friend, discussed the situation with a staff member, and prepared to go with dignity. Emily calmly got into line on the day her name was called and walked to the bus. As she approached the door, she quietly walked right on by—and nobody noticed. Later, when the buses were gone, she returned to her task, scrubbing steps in the building where she lived.

ITEM: On July 2, 1972, six young men drowned in the Missouri River while trying to save one another. Five were residents of a small-group home in Omaha, operated by the Eastern Nebraska Community Office of Retardation; the sixth was a dedicated, well-liked staff member.

On this long Fourth of July weekend, a group of staff members and citizens with handicaps who had become avid campers were fulfilling a long-sought wish to rough it at Indian Cave, Nebraska's newest state park. And all were experiencing a rich new high in their personal development—until the group began to wade in a large, placid-looking inlet of the Missouri River.

Then it happened! One man moved past an underwater ledge; he became caught in an undertow and was dragged down. Others went to his aid, only to find themselves also caught in the river's overpowering force. Some were pulled to safety, but when they saw others in trouble, they went back in again to help. Within five minutes, six men were lost, while the rest moved ashore, dazed and exhausted.

Six times during the next ten days, a body was found downstream; and six times a church or mortuary was packed, inside and out, with Omahans from all walks of life. There were friends (many with handicaps, who had known one another at institutions), relatives, neighbors, professionals, government officials, and volunteer workers—all drawn together by a common grief.

In the aftermath, many honored the staff member posthumously: The county board made a special award; a national convention of the Student Council for Exceptional Children was renamed as a memorial; statements about his courage were published—all more than deserved. He could have saved himself, but he did not.

However, after visiting the site of the tragedy, talking to staff members, attending six funerals, and listening to the other citizens with handicaps who were involved in the incident, a haunting question entered my mind: *Why did fewer people recognize heroism in the five men with handicaps?*

ITEM: In the late 1960s, Bengt Nirje created youth clubs throughout Stockholm. Each club contained twenty or fewer members—half were teen-agers with mental retardation; half were so-called normal adolescents. Many of the "normal" teen-agers had a brother or sister with a handicap. Each club carried out an ingenious unifying program called "hidden social training."[1] Two personal observa-

1. R. Perske, "The Dignity of Risk and the Mentally Retarded," *Mental Retardation*, vol. 10 (February 1972).

tions of instances of this training at work remain vivid in my mind. One Saturday, a youth club toured the Swedish National Theatre in downtown Stockholm. When the tour ended, each member was left to find his or her own way home *alone*—even if it meant asking questions of strangers, understanding directions, and finding the right bus or subway. Another Saturday, a club went on an outing to an amusement park. At a predetermined time, the so-called normal teenagers were "called away," leaving those with the handicaps to make choices and entertain themselves! In all fairness, however, one needs to take into account the general nonviolent attitude of the ordinary citizens of Stockholm, the respect they hold for persons with handicaps, and the thorough, competency-based training the nonhandicapped youth-club members underwent before they used the hidden social training concept in their own group.

ITEM: One set of parents, after taking a special course in "precision teaching" in Omaha, faced a painful fact. Even though their nine-year-old son had severe handicaps, they became aware that their "smothering" was contributing to his incontinence. With this new realization, and with the help of a professional who stayed at their home for three days, they developed a risky program. Each time James wet or dirtied his jeans, he was firmly but kindly taught to clean up his own mess. He cleaned the floor; put his soiled clothes in the washer and dryer; put on clean clothes. Later, he took the clothes out of the dryer, folded them and put them away. The program worked. Suddenly James realized that it was less work to put that stuff in the toilet than in his clothes. Although other children with the same problem might not be ready for such a risk—and that is why professional guidance is important—James learned to "overcorrect," make restitution, and pay the price for his own failure. Interestingly, when James achieved full control of his bodily excrements, he became just

as great a hero in his parents' eyes as did the others mentioned in this chapter.

These incidents lead to some interesting inferences.

Overprotection may appear on the surface to be kind, but it can be really evil. An oversupply can smother people emotionally, squeeze the life out of their hopes and expectations, and strip them of their dignity.

Overprotection can keep people from becoming all they could become.

Many of our best achievements came the hard way: We took risks, fell flat, suffered, picked ourselves up, and tried again. Sometimes we made it and sometimes we did not. Even so, we were given the chance to try. Persons with handicaps need these chances, too.

Of course, we are talking about *prudent* risks. People should not be expected to blindly face challenges that, without a doubt, will explode in their faces. Knowing which chances are prudent and which are not—this is a new skill that needs to be acquired.

On the other hand, a risk is real only when it is not known beforehand whether a person can succeed.

It is not so much the failure of courage in people with handicaps—it is that in the past, others have *prevented* them from being courageous. After all, if I act strong and heroic, something within me may forbid that I recognize one of *them* as a hero. However, the more I feel OK about people with handicaps and about myself, the less time I need to waste on such bluffs.

Today, you and I have renewed opportunities to search among the cowards of the world for heroes. After all, heroes are really cowards who "hung in there" longer than the rest of us. This time, with our new views, people with handicaps will be right up there on our list of heroes.

The real world is not always safe, secure, and predictable. It does not always say "please," "excuse me," or "I'm sorry." Every day we face the possibility of being thrown into situations where we will have to risk everything—perhaps even our lives. Therefore people with handicaps must be prepared—even hardened—for dangerous situations.

In the past, we found clever ways to build avoidance of risk into the lives of persons with handicaps. Now we must work equally hard to help find the proper amount of risk these people have the right to take. We have learned that there can be healthy development in risk taking . . . and there can be crippling indignity in safety!

Consider These Options

● The members of your immediate family can get together and agree on when the member with the handicap should be allowed to sink or swim . . . cry alone . . . be alone in the living room . . . move out of the yard . . .walk to a friend's house in the next block. Such risks could progress to buying groceries or taking a bus alone. All members in the family team can grow as they make fresh agreements daily about when they should protect their relative with the handicap, and when they should let him or her take a risk.

● Prepare for a surprise. Think of the persons with handicaps you know. Then think of the courageous acts you know they have carried out in their day-to-day living. Keep a running log to help you. You may be surprised by how many times these people outguess us and go beyond our expectations.

15. Relative Human Experience

Everyone struggles to achieve the good life. And those who think they have found it usually connect their success with . . .

overcoming personal problems

achieving personal goals

the amount of energy expended in the process.

For example, we all have known students who received "Excellents" and As on almost all their report cards. But for them, learning came easy. On the other hand, some of us worked extremely long hours to try to learn new concepts and pass examinations. We worked so hard that a single A was cause for a celebration.

If science ever develops a metering device which could be plugged into people to measure the ergs of energy they expend in achieving their goals, the world would have a clearer, more vivid definition of successful living. Until that time comes, a few persons I know—who happen to have developmental disabilities—make me wish that such a possibility were in the offing.

ITEM: Teen-ager Mary Washington sang some solo passages in a community youth chorus which had integrated a few persons with handicaps. She worked for weeks to memorize the words because she could not read. Then on the night she sang before a filled auditorium, she experienced the same thrill that you or I might know if we had sung the lead in a Broadway musical.

ITEM: Donald Shannon, a nine-year-old with atrophied legs, was learning to wheel his chair up a ramp. He worked at getting to the top for months, because he was promised the job as errand boy on the day he succeeded. When he made it, nearly thirty people gathered around him and applauded. On that day, it was obvious that Donald experienced the same thrill that you or I might enjoy if we had reached the summit of Mount Everest.

ITEM: On the night Martha and I were married, we held a supper celebration with a few friends at the Topeka Holiday Inn. During dinner, our waitress asked if an employee in the kitchen could come out and wish us well. On a night like this, why not? So out he came. The man's name was Ralph. He was about forty years old. I had known him five years earlier when he lived at the institution where I worked. (Sad to say, everybody there called him Ralphie—but nobody called him that now.) Ralph brought with him a wedding card with his name printed on it in large letters. My interest was aroused by meeting the man again after all these years, so he took me into the kitchen, showed me his dishwashing and pot-scrubbing station, and introduced me to his co-workers. It was clear that he was a valued member of that kitchen team and that he had had to overcome many fears and compensate for many disabilities to succeed at that job. Ralph saw his life as being good— very good! And I agreed.

As for that metering device . . . the one that can be plugged into people . . . the one that measures the ergs of energy people actually exert in achieving personal goals . . . it can't come too soon for me!

Consider These Options

- Take a fresh look at all the persons with handicaps you know about in your community.

- Try to look past where they are in life.

- Instead, try to sense how long and hard they had to work to get where they are.

- If you can do that, you will be among the growing number of people who hold special respect for certain dishwashers, busboys, hotel maids, shoeshiners, pieceworkers, and lawn workers—to name a few. You will come to see that all work has dignity . . . for someone.

- Do the same for those who struggle to gesture, speak, crawl, and reach out to you. You may never know when those milestones will prove to be monumental successes in their lives.

- In the meantime, come to grips with the fact that you will never fully understand Albert Einstein's explanation of relativistic dynamics as they exist in the nature of the universe and that you will never understand his mathematical expansions on the quantum theory. After all, Einstein was an extremely kind man, and he never would have held it against you if you could not function mentally on his level.

Margaret Ramirez and her eight-year-old son Jim walked out of the examining room at Denver's Children's Hospital. Her face was drawn and there was a quiet sadness in her eyes. Sensing that it was hard for her to speak, I suggested we get some coffee at the snack shop before making the drive back to her home in Sterling. We purchased our coffee—Jim wanted a bag of salted peanuts—and we sat down at a table. For awhile we sat in silence; even Jim sat quietly. Then it came.

"How much more does my kid have to take?" she said. "Hasn't he had enough?" She alluded to Jim's Down's Syndrome and the unbelievable number of crises he had weathered. There had been bouts with pneumonia, some painful incidents with neighborhood children, and a Logan County social worker's efforts to separate Jim from his mother and send him to an institution in Wheatridge.

Margaret told me what she had learned that morning: Jim's heart contained a hole between two chambers, causing him to experience periodic shortness of breath, headaches, and chest pains. The physicians had said he needed corrective surgery.

The mother poured it all out right in front of Jim. After all, it was 1956 and the principle of normalization had yet to arrive on the scene; we failed to be as considerate of his feelings as we would learn to be in later years.

During the conversation, we ignored what Jim was doing—that is, until we had to acknowledge what was taking place. This sharp, likable young man, fully aware of the trouble centering around him, had twisted up his usually smiling face into a serious frown. He had emptied the bag of peanuts on the table, and with determination, he had divided them, peanut by peanut, into three equal piles—one for his mother, one for me, and one for himself. Then with gracious sweeping movements, like a priest giving Communion, he placed our piles neatly beside our coffee cups.

Soon after, Jim did have his surgery, his uncomfortable symptoms ceased, and he grew to manhood in his own home.

Over the years, I lost contact with that mother and son. Now my most vivid memory of that day in Denver focuses on the way Jim—in the middle of *his* crisis—consciously chose to offer something to his mother and to me, as his attempt to alter the painful situation.

We always believed it was more blessed to give than to receive . . . as long as you were not handicapped. Then your giving became downright embarrassing to others. After all, because of your handicap, everybody should have been giving to you—or so we thought. This warped belief condemned hundreds with handicaps to be perpetually typecast as the suffering man lying beside the road . . . never as the Samaritan who came by, stopped, and gave help.

Today, we know better. Healthy living requires a high degree of giving, and those deprived of this option can become hopelessly crippled. Evidence to support this way of thinking is on the rise.

ITEM: Benny Savidis, a man with a thirty-two-year history of institutionalization, now grows beautiful tomatoes on a patch of ground behind his group home in Chicago. He produces enough for the home and gives the surplus away to six families on the block. Four other families have refused to accept his gifts, and Mr. Savidis has expressed sadness about this.

ITEM: Upon leaving a position in a Midwest institution, a seventeen-year-old resident—a longtime acquaintance—withdrew an item from his cigar-box treasure trove and handed it to me. It was a metal belt buckle bearing the national emblem of the Philippine Islands.

My first reaction was not to accept it. But I did, and it remains in my possession today.

Society usually sees children as receivers, and rightly so. Their survival depends upon it. Adults are more typically thought of as givers. Small wonder, then, that past views of persons with handicaps portrayed them as *eternal children*. The English journalist/advocate, Ann Shearer, cast additional light on this predicament a few years ago: "Mentally retarded persons are all too often caught in a half-world between childhood and adulthood, fitting into neither, frozen into a continuous state of becoming prepared to enter adult life, yet not enabled to reach it."[1]

It is possible that some persons with handicaps have not traversed this valley between childhood and adulthood because we have not permitted them to give to others and to the world as much as they are able to give.

Consider These Options

● Become tough-minded about not doing for your children with handicaps what they can do for themselves.

● Become even tougher-minded about being an unembarrassed but sensible receiver.

● Find regular, gracious, and natural ways to recognize and *reinforce* such acts of giving. Learn verbal and nonverbal ways to express appreciation: That was a thoughtful thing you did for me, son . . . What you did makes me love you all the more, daughter. . . . You make me glad you are in our family.

● Do not overdo your reinforcements. There can be times when our Good girl! and Good boy! can be so phony and loud we almost send our children sliding out of their chairs. Proper reinforcement is so important that some professionals study for doctorates, just to learn the right way to do it.

---

1. Speech given at Seventh World Congress of the International League of Societies for Persons with Mental Handicaps, Vienna, October, 1978.

17. Sexual Development

PERSKE

All human beings, handicapped or not, have their own rate of sexual growth embedded deep within their personalities. Healthy sexual development comes from . . .

being fed and held close in a loving mother's arms

being tickled and bounced on a father's knee

being hugged and shoved around by brothers and sisters

giving up body wastes at the right time and in the right place

becoming curious about all parts of one's own body

running, playing, and wrestling with friends in the neighborhood

girls making fun of boys

girls having their hair pulled

boys getting kicks in the shins from girls

having a best pal of the same sex

finding strange feelings in one's own genitals and discovering the pleasurable feelings one's own hands can produce

daring to go on a date

having a steady

feeling strange longings for someone of the opposite sex

feeling guilty for feeling that way

touching

wanting each other

deciding to have intercourse or to keep distance

discussing the consequences of togetherness

deciding to break up or to stay together

trying to understand what real love is

talking about marriage

making plans

breaking up

making plans

making commitments in a ceremony—or making agreements about an emotional partnership without a ceremony.

These experiences connected with physical and emotional partnerships between males and females really only scratch the surface. The list could continue into childbearing, raising children, separation from children, and living alone as couples in old age. Sexual experience begins at birth and continues until the day we die.

There is a problem, however, with sequential lists like these. They are too perfect. In real life, all of us have handled certain stages awkwardly and have failed to achieve others. (I have, but I refuse to tell you which ones.) If we managed all stages without fear, failure, or guilt, we probably would not be human at all—we would be machines.

Sex occupies our attention quite a bit these days because a sexual revolution is going on all around us.

Grandmother and grandfather, who were taught to avoid any mention of sex, are wondering what the world is coming to. Even so, we cannot be too judgmental of their old-fashioned views. When they were young—before penicillin and other modern drugs—venereal disease was horrible. And childbirth outside the sheltering family constellation, and without special government allotments, brought painful social and economic consequences.

The clergy often described sex as a temptation more powerful than a raging river. People were admonished to grit their teeth and keep those desires dammed up. Those who did let the dam break were seen as eternally soiled—the perpetrators of an unpardonable sin. Some clergy of the past were so tough on sex they took all the fun out of it—for the marrieds and unmarrieds alike.

Today, middle-aged persons sometimes work overtime in trying to make sense out of this revolution. Witness the hundreds of books on sexual development, the how-to-do-it-better manuals, and the sex therapy programs now available. Most are aimed at a middle-aged clientele: those born before the revolution began, who are trying to make up for what they missed.

Teen-agers are having a tough time, too. Theirs is the first generation that must try to build healthy emotional partnerships in an environment containing easy access to sexual knowledge, easy birth control, easy abortion, easy divorce (not really, except in a legal sense), and other easies as well.

Nevertheless, the sexual revolution can be beneficial to modern parents of persons with handicaps. Today, you can help unabashedly with the sexual development of your sons and daughters. No shame. No hiding it. You can help them attain their most genuine possible level of functioning. Best of all, you can be more relaxed and considerate in the process than ever before.

It has not always been this way. Some years ago, we literally tried to stamp sexuality out of the lives of persons with handicaps. Henry Goddard and his colleagues, mentioned earlier, felt that sex and persons with handicaps should be separated—even brutally if necessary. In *The Kallikak Family* he argued for a scrupulously monitored division of the sexes within institutional colonies, ovariectomies for females, and castration for males. Obviously, many who supervised these people agreed.

Most institutions of the past were built so that dormitories for males and females were situated on opposite sides of large grassy expanses. Men and women were together in places such as dining halls, but even there they sat apart from one another and were never beyond the watchful eyes of caretakers. All longings for close friendships with the opposite sex were blocked.

In Nebraska, it was not until 1968 that the state legislature repealed a law calling for the sterilization of females before discharge from state institutions.

Between 1894 and 1944, in a Kansas institution, hundreds of males with developmental disabilities were castrated. The care-fully kept records of these surgical interventions showed that many took place as a measure to stop a "nameless habit," which today we openly call masturbation.

Now we are learning that it was our aberrant knowledge about *our own* sexuality that became amplified and was projected on others—especially those with handicaps. We know better now. We have new opportunities to handle sexual myths, fears, and obsessions without dumping them on the backs of those unable to fight back.

Nevertheless, human sexuality still remains an extremely complex subject—as complex as individuals themselves. A response to one child in a specific situation may be all wrong when dealing with another. We begin our own inimitable sexual development just as we would begin to play chess, learning a few appropriate rules. But we actually learn the game by playing it—by using our best thinking, making moves, and learning from mistakes.

In regard to masturbation, parents at one time recited horrible, picturesque stories, some of them handed down from earlier generations, about what happened to adolescents who indulged in it. Now, however, masturbation receives a more acceptable place in the lineup of sexual activities. Most members of society feel it is all right to masturbate, providing it is done discreetly and in private. Some people not able to reach responsible heterosexual intercourse may use masturbation as an alternate release of sexual tensions. Of course, the functioning of others may be at a level which keeps them from achieving a masturbation stage. If so, this fact will have to be accepted.

But what about marriage? Are some persons too handicapped for such emotional partnerships? Of course. And some may be working so hard to overcome less sophisticated barriers that they simply do not have time or interest in the opposite sex. I still chuckle about a course on sexuality I taught to a group of teenagers in an institution in 1964. One of my most promising students wanted out when he learned that on a date, he was expected to buy the female's movie ticket. Another young man, after we had discussed the names and functions of male and female genitals, simply asked, "Can't I just be friends with a girl without messing around with all this put-it-together stuff?" After seeing a film on childbirth and talking about raising children, some members of the class openly admitted that they did not feel up to making and raising a baby. Fortunately, recent programs which explore closeness and distances between males and females are leading many with handicaps to make their own responsible decisions about relationships with the opposite sex.

Some persons with handicaps are achieving successful marriages today. Most, however, received special training and ongoing support from a new breed of professionals, parents, and advocates. For example, in the spring of 1979, the Columbia Broadcasting Company presented a two-hour television special, "No Other Love," a touching story of a man and a woman with mental retardation who fell in love and were married. One month later, the American Broadcasting Company also aired a feature about a similar marriage. ABC's presentation, "Like Normal People," was based on the book with the same title (New York: McGraw-Hill, 1978) by *Washington Post* reporter Robert Meyers, who wrote about the marriage of his brother. Both specials received high audience ratings and national awards.

Since such possibilities would have been utterly unthinkable ten years earlier, what has made such options available for today? There have been many influencing factors.

Regular Family Experiences. Many persons with handicaps now grow up in their own families. The social crippling that can come from living in isolated, overcrowded, super-regimented institutions was never a part of their experience.

The Right to Love a Person of the Opposite Sex. Forward-thinking parents, professionals, and ordinary citizens do indeed recognize this human right. And this does not necessar-

ily mean the right to love *only* another person with a handicap. The best-selling novel *Tim*, by Coleen McCullough (New York: Popular Library, Fawcett Books, 1974), emphasizes this fact.

Sophisticated Community-Living Training Programs. Success in cooking, housekeeping, grooming, working, receiving salaries, budgeting, shopping, choosing apparel, behaving appropriately in the community, living alone or semi-independently, and riding public transportation has opened the lives of persons with handicaps to other new vistas— such as falling in love and developing emotional partnerships with those of the opposite sex.

Formal Sex Education. Today sex-education programs are conducted in all enlightened service agencies for persons with handicaps. Robert Meyers commented on the training his brother and sister-in-law received: "Roger and Virginia knew about sex, about intercourse, about orgasms, about pregnancy, and about everything else that people in their twenties knew about."

Some professionals in the field have become so competent that they actually assist in the act of intercourse until independently controlled prosthetic devices can be managed by those with physical handicaps, or until a tender understanding of the other partner's needs can be gained and protection of the other partner can be mastered.

Although there is no evidence that such a program ever has been carried out in North America, Uruguay has reported a program for screening and training a select number of prostitutes in understanding persons with handicaps, in order for them to engage in the first act of intercourse with those persons. The rationale for such a program was given by a Uruguayan physician at the Fifth International Congress on Mental Retardation in Montreal (International League of Societies for Persons with Mental Handicaps, October 1972). According to her, "We feel it is important that this first experience be healthy, thoughtful, and pleasurable—to make sure that their first experience is a good one." It is doubtful that such a program would harmonize with the culture and morals of North American communities. Nevertheless, facts about things happening elsewhere in the world need not be hidden from your view.

Quality Pastoral Counseling and Guidance. There was a day when all pastoral problems connected with persons having developmental disabilities were referred to institutional chaplains. Not so today. Quality programs, entailing many hours of counseling and preparations for formal marriages are being carried out across the continent by certain clergy who have a special interest in those with handicaps. Some of these sessions, based on the responses of the marriage candidates, skillfully lead toward a formal ceremony . . . others lead away.

Ongoing Professional and Advocacy Supports. More and more community agencies are providing in-home supports for married couples with handicaps. Robert Meyers described the ongoing support given by the counselor who worked with his brother and sister-in-law.

> Quietly and with infinite patience, she listens to Roger and Virginia . . . and struggles with them as they attempt to express their thoughts. Carol makes suggestions on everything from menu planning to appropriate clothing for different occasions, and in subtle ways, she helps them steer themselves to a more normal life.

Any marriage is a risky undertaking. It can be a madhouse, or it can lead to the most nurturing, life-stabilizing partnership two humans can experience. Or it can be somewhere in between.

Also, there is no hard evidence to show that when persons with handicaps marry, the results are any better or worse than those of so-called normal persons. The time has come for persons with handicaps to experience the dignity that comes from considering these risks, too.

Consider These Options

● Settle in your mind as quickly as you can that sex education at its very best is not an academic short course. It is a lifelong training program that begins at birth.

● Understand that no professional or advocate can teach your child about sex as thoroughly and as richly as you can.

● Develop skill in recognizing periodic opportune moments for helping your child acquire genuine sexual knowledge. These occasions arise when small boys take showers with small girls . . . when children ask why a woman's stomach is so big . . . when they ask what certain words mean . . . when they want to know why they are different from those of the opposite sex.

● Help your child learn the most valuable fact of all: *It is sexual intercourse that causes babies to be born.* As soon as your child is able to get this fact into his or her head, do not cloud it with awkward silences, never minds, we-will-talk-about-it-laters, and unbelievable stories about storks, cabbage leaves, and watermelon seeds.

● If and when your child does understand what intercourse can do, then emphasize the next most important fact: Engaging in an act that enables babies to be born is serious business—something that requires a heavy responsibility.

● If the day comes when your son or daughter tries to decide whether to have a baby, you might suggest the following: Invite him or her to help care for someone else's infant for two weeks. Then help the couple to make the decision. (This advice might make sense for the rest of us, too.)

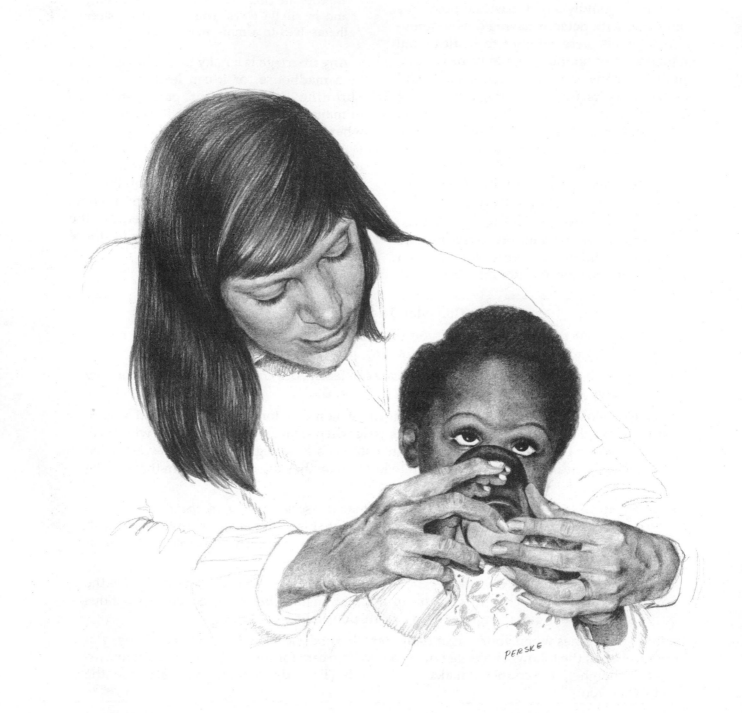

PERSKE

Thirty years ago, so little money was provided to help persons with developmental disabilities that nobody bothered to keep an accurate account. In 1980, however, different levels of government in Canada and in the United States spent more than twenty-five billion dollars for this purpose. Three decades of hard work had paid off.

Of course, this increase was influenced by . . .

    organized parent task forces
    new breakthroughs by technicians
    increased skills in professionals
    volunteer-advocacy efforts
    self-advocacy impacts
    coordinated lobbying strategies
    individualized program planning
    energizing ideologies
    persuasive public-attitude-change efforts
    landmark court cases.

But while we worked, something else had begun to happen. Ordinary citizens and public officials began to grow up in their thinking. They began to see persons with handicaps as . . .

    developing persons
    real people
    loyal friends
    struggling heroes
    and most important of all,
    as good as the next person.

In other words, the common-garden-variety citizen and official began to see persons with handicaps as *valued individual human beings* with weaknesses and strengths, just like the rest of us. And although it never could be traced directly, those three decades of programmatic sweating and anguishing by committed parents, professionals, and advocates have been influencing the collective consciousness of neighborhoods throughout North America. Great! This general change of heart in the community carries a convincing wallop when there is a vote to fund programs for persons with handicaps.

I believe there is a definite correlation between a community's *views* of such people and the money it *invests* in them. In short, we are spending more because we value them more.

Consider These Options

● Know that your close proximity to your neighbors puts you in an excellent position to help them develop healthy attitudes toward your child with developmental disabilities.

● Set a personal goal to help your immediate neighbors see value in your child. How you go about this may vary from neighbor to neighbor, but set the goal consciously.

● Believe with all your heart that truly decent neighborhoods see all their children—handicapped or not—as the real wealth of the world.

Although the widening world of childhood contains hundreds of lessons delivered by parents and teachers, young people deliver powerful lessons to one another, too. Small children are uncanny about teaching each other "the ropes" to acceptable childhood living. For example, I recall seven-year-old Bob McGee, with mental retardation and cerebral palsy, who fell to the floor kicking and screaming every time a teacher tried to take off his bib. Then when the developmental center closed down and Bob was transferred to a special class in a regular public school, he had attended for only two days before the bib came off! It takes little imagination to know what probably went on between him and the other students.

Teen-agers perform rich informal functions in teaching one another what life is all about and how they want their generation to shape the world. Although this curriculum cannot be found in books, teen-agers share with each other their own . . .

    values
    clothing styles
    meaningful slang words
    sense of justice
    choice of foods
    hope for the future
    even their anger for mistakes their elders
      made before them.
    (Have you forgotten?)

Until recently, many children with handicaps were denied peer-group interactions with others their own age. Like victims of apartheid, they attended special schools, rode special buses, and participated in special recreation programs. Of course, such distinctive activities had value, and there always will be a need for some specialized programs. Nevertheless, such utter isolation produced tragic consequences. It placed one more barrier in their path to the richest life possible. Now this unfair obstacle is being lowered.

Today many preschools integrate children with developmental disabilities into classes with their "normal" peers. And what often goes on in such settings can enlighten us all. A documentary film, *Why Be Friends*, described integrated preschools in eastern Nebraska. "Normal" children spoke openly and in unrehearsed fashion about their friends with handicaps. One four-year-old was asked about her relationship with a friend having multiple handicaps.

"What's that thing behind Carrie's head?"
"That's the thing that holds her head."
"Why does she have to have that?"
"Because then her head won't do anything, but it helps her lean back a lot."
"How would you feel if Carrie couldn't come here to school?"
"Well, then I'd go to her house."

Experiences like these in integrated preschools teach us that prejudice against persons with handicaps is *learned* behavior. And if prejudice can be taught by what we elders say (or fail to say), then tolerance, respect, and love for those with disabilities can be taught, too.

Forward-thinking public schools recognize the power of peer-group education. Dr. Lou Brown from the University of Wisconsin, which has close training relationships with the Madison Metropolitan School District, gave a touching rationale for such involvements at one of the symposiums on the United Nations' International Year of the Child (1979). He felt that neighborhood children should relate to students with even severe and profound handicapping conditions.

Children with severe and profound handicaps need to be in regular schools, too. This interaction between these handicapped students and other students is utterly remarkable. And why not? After all, the future parents of such handicapped children are in the schools today. And what kind of attitudes, values and expectations will such parents need? Also, future doctors, teachers, lawyers, policemen and ministers are in the schools, too. They need to grow up with such children so they will understand them and not reject them. Therefore, we are making conscious and systematic attempts to make sure that every student has some kind of interaction with such handicapped people. And in some schools I work closely with, we train regular students to handle seizures in school . . . to work with handicapped students at recess, in the gym and the swimming pool . . . to hire out as baby sitters for handicapped children . . . to help some learn to ride the bus . . . to wheel students in wheelchairs to and from school. In many cases, regular students receive class credit for their involvements with handicapped persons. These students have become so attracted to one another, we can't keep them apart.[1]

Harold Howe II, the former United States Commissioner of Education and present vice president of Education and Research at the Ford Foundation, believes strongly that peer-group education will become a new way of life in public schools by A.D. 2024. He stated, "What the schools increasingly reward is not the student's own achievement but his contribution to the achievement of others. And the higher his own attainments in learning, the more he is expected to do in helping others to learn."[2]

It will happen. We can slow it down, however, as long as we keep people with handicaps apart from the rest of us.

Consider These Options

● Become interested in remarkable relationships between persons with handicaps and so-called normal persons in your neighborhood. They form the stuff books and speeches are made of. I make a living from such happenings—maybe you can observe relationships worth writing or talking about, too.

● Know that life becomes exciting and the world moves forward when people with individual differences understand and accept each other. After all, when we associate only with those who think like we do, act like we do, dress like we do, talk like we do—well, it can get downright boring.

● Watch your local public schools. Every time you see them develop a program that even smells like peer-group education involving persons with handicaps, reinforce them. Send written thank yous. Submit letters to editors. Thank the persons responsible personally. Even hug them and kiss them, if you can get away with it.

● Know that peer-group education is a coming way of life. It *is* coming. It is up to us to develop detailed responses that will help it along.

---

1. Robert Perske, ed., *The Child with Retardation—The Adult of Tomorrow: An International Year of the Child Report Sponsored by the International League of Societies for the Mentally Handicapped and the Association for Retarded Citizens* (Arlington, Tex.: ARC-National Headquarters, 1980).
2. Harold Howe, "Report to the President of the United States from the Chairman of the White House Conference on Education, August 1, 2024," *Saturday Review World* (August 24, 1974).

20. Family Systems

When a man and a woman come together in marriage, both change their life-styles—or they ought to. They build a new give-and-take system of two. When the arrangement works well, both are better off than when they lived alone. When the system functions badly, life becomes worse than before.

When a baby or other relative enters the picture, the family needs to grow into a mutually nurturing system of three. And so it goes for the families of four, five, or more.

When one member of the system has a handicap, the process is exactly the same. And in all fairness, the person with the disability may not be the most difficult member of the family system. On the other hand, specific problems brought on by handicaps need to be faced before the one with the handicap becomes a regular family member.

Many things could be said about family systems, but only a few will appear here—a few simple facts you need to know.

There is no such thing as an ideal family system. There are only messy ones, containing different combinations of weaknesses and strengths. Of course, in their minds, professionals do create perfect family systems, and they write books about them. Fine, if the systems in their minds serve only as models. But if they lead you to believe that such perfect relationships actually exist, they are being unfair.

Only one family system like yours exists. It is incomparable. It is unique. Consequently . . .

you read a book or magazine article describing the healthy family and often end by feeling inadequate (I do)

you listen to someone lecture on family life and you come away feeling you are an utter failure as a parent (same here)

you fill out one of those take-this-simple-test-to-see-how-your-family-rates examinations that appear in newspapers and popular magazines; after scoring it, the rating chart tells you that your family relationships fall into the "deficient" classification (mine always do).

Why does this happen? Because the author, lecturer, or examiner had another family in mind.

Society has programmed families to reject children with developmental problems. If your family moved to a secluded island and you lived alone, like the *Swiss Family Robinson*, you might find it easier to work your child with the handicap into your family. Or if yours were a pioneer family, with everyone committed to clearing the land, planting, hunting, and trapping, you might see a certain child as not being handicapped at all. Sometimes it is not you, but the views of those around you that can mess up your family system. In the past, professionals even had a hand in such activities. A recent report to the President documents this fact.

> Parents of older mentally retarded persons can tell of harrowing experiences in the not-too-distant past when they requested help from health, education and welfare professionals. Often, the only answer they received was: "Send him to an institution." One pediatrician in Washington state recently commented, "When I reminisce about how we, the professionals, used to deal with such families, it strikes me that we were utterly brilliant at separating mothers and fathers from their mentally retarded children." Such "brilliance" still exists today, of course, but it is definitely diminishing. (Perske, *Mental Retardation: The Leading Edge*.)

Although the presidential report cited a grim past, it ended with a hopeful conclusion.

Incentives to Families. More and more agencies and governments are creating incentives that influence families to keep their mentally retarded children within their own homes. These incentives are replacing the financial and social incentives which for years have motivated parents to send their children away to institutions.

Some family systems become stronger. Some do, but some do not. One family's challenge is another's albatross. At any rate, some do draw closer around a member with a handicap, and because they do, they achieve more robust ways of perceiving and of living in the world than they had ever dreamed of before persons with the handicap entered their circle. But really, when you think about it, the same thing happens—to a greater or lesser degree—when grandparents, aunts, uncles, hired hands, and even newborn babies with no apparent problems move into the system.

Parents influence the directions of the family system. That is, they should. If small children control the family's general attitudes and actions, that family could be in big trouble. Healthy growth in children involves the *internalizing* of the best views and responses of their parents. Therefore children do pick up cues which influence their attitudes toward a brother or sister with disabilities.

A sense of humor helps. Times can get tough.

And believe it or not, laughter and humor of the right kind can help a family get through such periods. Of course, the problems you will face can never be minimized. But when things are grim, there is a tendency to become tight, rigid, and unbending. Such tightness can cripple a warm growth process in a family. A playful attitude on the part of all the members can help keep your system operating at its best.

The systems concept is great for selling encyclopedias throughout North America; making sugar out of beets in Sterling, Colorado; developing oil fields in Fort McMurray, Alberta; landing a Boeing 727 at La Guardia Airport; or defending a nation with an elaborate array of intercontinental ballistic missles. But even these arrangements—based on pure science—can experience earth-shaking shifts caused by a wily little rascal called the *human factor*.

When the systems concept is applied to family relationships, especially those like yours, the human factor increases many times. Good! Families do not operate like machines. So dare to be unpredictable . . . let your humanness come through. Do the best you can. That is all you can be expected to do.

Consider These Options

● Make a list of all the families you know that are stronger because a person with a handicap lives within their system. Then without disparaging anyone, make a confidential list of the families you feel are worse off. Ponder the results.

● Think of all the times families of members with handicaps have made you laugh at their description of a crucial human situation they had experienced.

● Discover mechanisms within yourself, and reinforce mechanisms within other members of your family, which will enable you to laugh at tough situations your system must face. Of course, the mechanisms will not work every time. But when they do, let them.

● Stop comparing your family with other families; stop feeling yours must always be like others.

● Make a big deal out of the fact that there is only one family like yours. Enjoy your uniqueness! Be proud of it.

Today when people get out of tune with one another, they often play "games." According to one popular school of psychology, they play games for a variety of reasons: to avoid confronting reality, to conceal ulterior motives, to rationalize their activities, or to avoid actual participation. Although some games are harmless and even helpful, others are destructive.

Families of persons with handicaps can play games, too. Here are some they should be careful not to play.

He-Broke-Us-Up. Husbands and wives play this game. All appears to be going well until a child with a handicap enters the family. Then the husband-wife relationship gets worse and worse until it ends in separation and divorce. Everyone observing the process is led to believe that the presence of the child caused the split. Actually, hidden seeds of mistrust and dislike already were present, and the presence of the child served only as an excuse for cultivating those quiet little hates.

The worst payoff in such a game comes later . . . the child may go through life feeling, "I must really be a bad person if my being born shattered my mom and dad's marriage."

The introduction of a child, handicapped or "normal," cannot break up a good family system. For the most part, husband and wife must take the responsibility for the positive or the negative direction of their marriage.

The-One-Who-Isn't-There. I recall when Jack, age fourteen, was asked by a psychologist to draw a picture of his family. He drew his mother, father, brother, and sister. But he did not draw himself in the picture. At some levels, he was not an accepted member of that family. Although the family took care of his basic needs, they ignored him as a contributing member with his own ideas, hopes, risks, and urges to be needed.

One day when his mother was in the hospital for surgery, Jack did some work at his church and earned enough money to buy flowers. Then during visiting hours, he walked into the hospital room with the flowers, accompanied by the pastor. His mother and the rest of the family greeted him, almost in unison: "What are you doing here?"

He's-Our-Master. If you were a foreigner from the planet Ork, watching a family play this game without understanding their language, you would observe the following: A small person screams; everyone runs toward him. He shouts again; the largest woman gets something and puts it in his mouth. He overturns a chair; the tall man comes to him smiling and says soothing things while setting up the chair. He pulls on the curtain; two of the smaller people appear front-and-center and take him for a walk. After watching this process, you, with your Orkian mind, say to yourself, "Such power; that little one is the most powerful leader I have ever seen. His subjects comply with his every command."

Any child, handicapped or not, who can control the rest of the family that way is not really a regular member of that family. And the most damaging effect of such a game is that the child never will become acquainted with the real world in which he must someday live. In no other place on earth will people be at his beck and call.

It's-His-Fault. Every time a failure or defeat comes to any family member who plays this game, he or she automatically points a finger toward the person with the handicap. "I didn't make cheerleader because my brother is retarded." (This may be easier to say than "I didn't do as well as the other girls.") "Sally turned me down for a date because my brother is deformed and rolling around in that wheelchair." (This may be easier to believe than "Sally doesn't like me enough to go out with me.") "If only we didn't have Jim, they would have made me general manager."

(This belief causes less pain than facing the fact that someone else was more qualified.) When finger pointing like this takes place in a family, a person with a handicap becomes a convenient household appliance for collecting blames. Healthy families do not have such catchalls. They are not needed.

Walking-Pharmaceutical-House. Every time family members in authority feel nervous or bothered and want to be left alone, they give medicine to the one with the handicap. Of course, the complaint to the prescription-writing physicians describes the person with the handicap as being hyperactive and nervous. Sometimes the complaint is accurate. But in some cases, it is others who are nervous and high strung. Every family member should take his or her own medicine, rather than drugging the one with a handicap into a zombielike stupor.

There Are Other Games. After catching on to the knack of it, you can think of other games . . .
　　There's-Nothing-Wrong-with-Him
　　He's-Better-with-His-Own-Kind
　　If-You-Don't-Do-Something-I'll-Get-Sick
　　It-Is-Your-Genes-That-Are-Rotten
　　Push-Me-and-the-Kid-Gets-a-Seizure.

Consider These Options

● Give names to the games you catch yourself playing—those that permit you to avoid facing tough problems.

● Help other family members give names to their puzzling maneuvers, too.

● Let the names be as humorous as possible. Laugh at them as much and as often as you can.

● Think of the games you could play, but do not. My hunch is that you might be able to develop quite a list.

---

22. Brothers and Sisters

PERSKE

Attention brothers and sisters: Most of these words have been written with you in mind, too. It just happens that your mothers and fathers were around long before you were, so it made sense to get the book into their hands first. Now, however, if you find this book lying around the house, feel free to put the words *brother* or *sister* in place of *parents,* and read it yourself.

On the other hand, a few things need to be said directly to you.

I was a little brother, so it is only fair to remind you that big sisters and brothers have strong needs to prove that little ones are noxious little asses who should be done in. I am sure their first experiences of evil in the world focused on little ones like me. At least that is what I gathered from my big sister's statements: "Why do we have to have *him* in the family?" and "I love everybody in the whole world except for the devil and my little brother." (All that, just because it was fun to do things like putting grasshoppers down her back?) On the other hand, we little ones often saw big brothers and sisters as overwhelming powers of darkness who would get us if we did not move fast enough. We learned the true meaning of "the *quick* and the dead."

But there is love between brothers and sisters, too. Good love. Stick-up-for-one-another love. Be-kind-to-him-when-he's-sick love. Teach-her-what-to-watch-out-for-in-the-neighborhood love. Of course, brothers and sisters do not show their love for one another as adult lovers do. (Thank goodness for that.) But a good love can be present.

Parents are not the only ones who shape us; brothers and sisters do, too. We fight, care, share, shame, support, and we survive—these interactions help us develop the proper balance of hardness and softness as adults. So believe it or not, brothers and sisters can be good for one another.

But what about brothers and sisters with handicaps? There was a day when many physicians told parents to send children away to institutions. The reason: If they stayed at home, their brothers or sisters would suffer harmful effects. Doctors usually do not say things like that anymore. But it is something you need to ponder—your parents, too.

In the April 1972 edition of *Psychology Today*, an article by Frances Grossman, "Brothers and Sisters of Retarded Children," presented the results of a study of the effects of such a situation on eighty-three college students, each of whom had a brother or sister with retardation. How many were harmed by the experience? How many were stronger? Half and half. She stated:

> Our final tabulations revealed a number of subjects who appeared to have benefited from the experience of growing up with handicapped siblings. . . . The ones who benefited appeared to us to be more tolerant, more compassionate, more knowing about prejudice and its consequences and they were often, but not always, more certain about personal and vocational goals, than comparable young adults who had not had such experiences.
>
> The ones we judged to have been harmed often manifested bitter resentfulness of their families' situations, guilt about the rage they had felt at their parents and at the retarded sibling, and fear that they themselves might be defective. Often they had been deprived of attention that they needed to help them develop, simply because so much family time and energy had been given to the handicapped children.

Of course, those college students were born in the early 1960s, and society was rougher on persons with handicaps then. Maybe a later study would produce different results . . . or would it?

It appears that the presence of a brother or sister with a handicap in your family puts extra ingredients—good and bad—into your life, which can teeter you toward becoming either stronger or weaker. It may be, however, that you already were leaning in that direction. The only difference: This situation teetered you farther. Be that as it may, two needs remain clear.

You, too, are a valuable, developing, individual human being. You, too, need to be recognized, to be loved, and to develop into the best person you can be.

Your brother or sister with the handicap needs to experience the most robust, risky, rough-but-kind interactions with you that he or she can tolerate—as close to normal sibling relationships as possible.

Usually, the two needs go hand in hand. Sometimes, however, for reasons you can control, or for reasons you can't (parents influence the situation, too), the two options clash. If so, I hope you do the best you can.

Above all, be yourself. There are no such people as superbrothers or supersisters, but there are no superficial ones, either. You count, too.

Consider These Options

● If you read this section, discuss it with your parents. Let them know how you feel. Maybe you can have some good discussions.

● If you have younger brothers and sisters, and if you think you have a healthy outlook on the situation, share it with them. Put it into words they can understand.

● Look around for others who have brothers and sisters with handicaps. If it feels OK to compare notes and learn from each other, do it.

---

23. Healthy Launching Pads and Proper Landing Fields

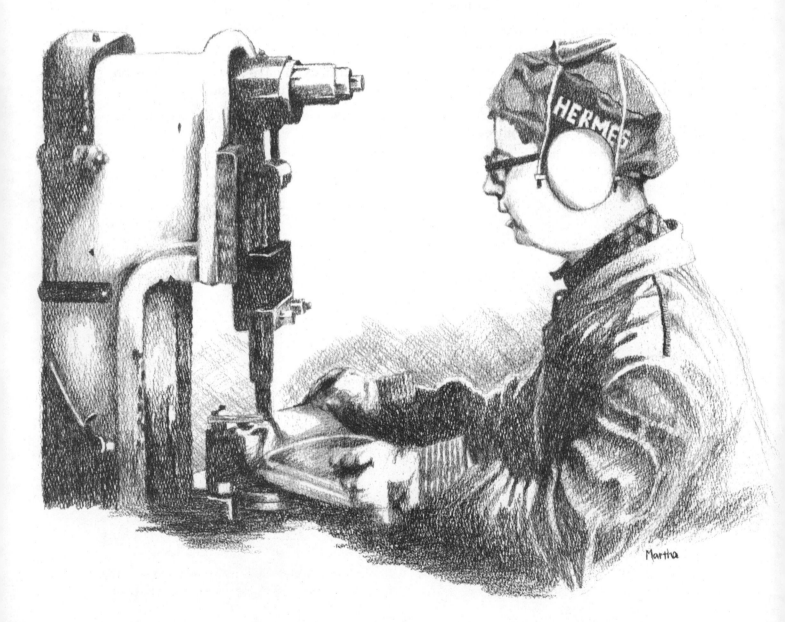

Martha

Earlier in the history of North America, most people lived on farms and ranches, and their families operated as interdependent "extended-kin" systems. When the children grew up, they often stayed at home; they earned their keep by doing their fair share of the work. By doing so, they added to the larger-family income. Even uncles, aunts, grandparents, and cousins moved in and became a productive part of some family systems. A robust arrangement. Now, however, those days are gone forever for most children.

Today the family economy makes it impossible for most sons and daughters to stay at home after reaching adulthood. And since breaking away can be painfully complicated, it happens in different ways.

Some leave in a storm, saying "I can't take living in this boring place any longer" or "I've had it with everybody meddling in my private affairs." And away they go. Later, however, when they make it on their own, they often look back on the homestead with love and respect.

Some go to out-of-town jobs or on trips that appear too exotic to pass up.

Others go to college or into the armed forces, knowing that when they graduate or separate from the service, they will not return home.

Some flee the home by diving blindly into marriage. Fewer young people use this means of emancipation now—they may have come to believe that Shakespeare was right when he said, "It is better to be well-hung than to be ill-wed."

Of course, others discuss the situation openly with their parents; they recognize the natural course of events and calmly move out. But even such rational separations may bring on sick feelings in stomachs, sleepless nights, cold sweats, and bouts of downright sadness and tears.

When sons and daughters hang around too long, parents may resort to other rational or irrational ways to boot them out of the nest.

In all fairness, you need to know that some sons and daughters still do stay at home, that they have good reasons for doing so, and that they live full lives, just as in the extended-kin families of the past. But usually, because of economic problems, most children must move out. Consequently, the modern family serves as a launching pad. And the process of preparing children to live away from home begins at birth.

Up to this point, our focus has been on so-called normal children. But what about those with handicaps? Face it. The complications are greater. After all, children with handicaps, being more dependent on their parents, usually have to go through greater anguish before they finally determine to announce—either calmly or in a huff—their intention to move out. Of course, some can never do it. And parents—after years of extra protecting, guiding, and reinforcing—go through anguish, too, before pushing them out. The world out there is often heartless and tough. I think that even mother robins must hesitate to shove out a child with disfigured wings. After all, what good is a successful launch when you know it will end in a crash?

Be that as it may, know that while you read these words, others are working on proper "landing fields" for persons with handicaps. In communities throughout Canada and the United States, parents like you, professionals, and volunteer advocates are locking arms, planning, lobbying, and literally fighting for community-based service systems. Here are some of the programs they are creating and their possibilities for you.

Early Intervention. The moment you learn that your child possesses a developmental disability—even if it is at birth—he or she needs special developmental services immediately. Remember, a good preparation for adult life does begin at birth.

Family Supports. Unlike parents of persons with handicaps in the past, you should never be forced to go it alone. There must be competent counseling and guidance at your disposal. You also need at least one emergency telephone number for immediate help, day or night. You need financial supports, too.

Respite Care. You need a certain number of hours per week to get away on your own —the exact amount depends upon the severity of your child's handicap. In most cases, competency-based respite-care workers should come to your home and stay with your child. This gives you a breather and your child an early beginning in interaction with others from the outside world.

Public School Education. Your child needs a full-service public-school education geared to his or her specific needs. Such education should focus on hundreds of skills, ranging from swallowing properly to living alone successfully. Except for a few persons with intense medical problems and those having early in-home programs, this education should take place in regular public-school buildings.

Public-Attitude Change. It is not enough that your attitude toward your child change. Programs for changing the attitude of citizens in your community should receive constant attention.

Community Residences. At the proper time, your son or daughter should move into a home that is tailor-made for his or her specific developmental needs. The home might be a twenty-four-hour intensive-care residence, private family where the adults are trained developmentalists, a family-scale group home, an apartment with live-in staff, a semi-independent apartment, or a house or apartment where your son or daughter eventually will live alone.

Adult Day-Activities. Of course, landing a full-time job is the ideal. But those unable to reach this goal need dignified, age-appropriate alternatives—activities tailor-made to fit their actual developmental levels.

Leisure-Time Activities. Your son or daughter needs a variety of relaxing or invigorating off-time opportunities, just as the rest of us do. The more these amusements, sports, and hobbies take place with "normal" people, and the more they are provided by the managers of regular facilities, the better.

Adult Education. Development does not stop at age twenty-one. In fact, many persons with handicaps have a greater need for learning in their twenties than ever before. Therefore continuing education—night school or special community-college experiences—needs to be available to your son or daughter throughout his or her adult life.

Advocates. Since your offspring may not always speak up for himself or herself as well as other citizens can, trained volunteers and professionals are needed from time to time to represent his or her interests. Advocacies can take many forms: one-to-one friendships; advocacies for crisis situations; legal advocacies when rights are being violated. Some advocate tasks may involve no personal contact at all (e.g., a businessman who periodically checks a bank account for accurate bookkeeping, overdrafts and underspending; a medical professional who checks records for overmedication; an educator who makes periodic checks on an education plan).

Self-advocacy. When one advocates for another, it is good, but when one speaks out successfully for one's self, it is better. Your son or daughter needs to speak up for himself or herself as much as possible. Recently, persons with handicaps began to organize to help one another do exactly that. Most of these organizations do use professional and volunteer "helpers" (the so-called normal persons in the group), chosen because they have the good sense to know when to shut up and let people with handicaps struggle to solve their own problems.

Just as an artist begins by outlining a canvas with a broad brush, so these community program components are described in general terms. Although few existed twenty years ago, now each contains hundreds of neighborhood-inspired variations—so many, in fact, that experts write complete books about each type.

Nevertheless, as yet no community in North America possesses all the necessary components in its own community service system—only bits and pieces. But people are working on these systems as never before in the history of the world. Persons with handicaps do need to be nurtured in healthy launching pads, but they also need to land in communities that are ready for their arrival.

Consider These Options

• Browse the list of general community-service components. Determine which one is most needed now by your son or daughter. Does your neighborhood have such a program? If so, is it adequate? If either of these questions receives a negative answer, make a written list of steps you think you could carry out during the next twelve months to help get that service—or to improve the existing one—in your community.

• Become a community-service expert. Many parents work toward this goal . . . they have to. After all, you are a consumer—or the representative of a consumer—and you know, better than most, what programs are needed and whether they are working well.

• Look around for other experts like yourself. Compare notes. An amazing power can be developed when four or five of you get together and really click.

• Ponder your son or daughter's *presence* in the community. Is it enough? If not, make a written list of things you personally can do within one year to make your child's presence known.

• Consider your child's *participation* in the community. (Being present is good, but participating is important, too.) If you feel your son or daughter's participation should increase, write down a list of things your child could do to be more involved.

---

24. Parent/Professional Relationships

In the past, parents did not always feel comfortable with professionals. Gail Stigen, a professional, and the parent of a child with developmental disabilities, wrote an extremely humorous book, *Heartaches and Handicaps* (Palo Alto, Cal.: Science & Behavior Press, 1976) which focused on this issue. Among her many hilarious descriptions of parent/professional encounters was this sketch of her first session with a social worker.

> Suddenly, I became aware of this person standing next to me. . . . I got up to look into the face of this elegantly turned-out person who was watching us with no expression. What I had at first perceived to be a store dummy finally asked if I was her nine o'clock appointment. I quickly checked my driver's license to remember my name, which I blurted out before I forgot it. It was conveyed to me that I should follow this humanoid. . . .
>
> There followed a scene only an overtrained professional can stage manage. When we entered her office (with me trailing as due my inferior role), the door was firmly closed and my Social Worker sat down behind her desk in her Executive Swivel Chair. At first I thought I had been forgotten. What seemed like hours went by as she perused an impressive file, while I stood there like a lump, my shoes pointed inward, and I fought an overwhelming urge to whistle or hum. . . .
>
> The office was shoe-box shaped and not much bigger. My razor-sharp mind told me that there was no chair for me and I realized immediately that we were going to have quite an informal session, with me either on the floor (as in Girl Scouts) or perched on her desk (as at the office Xmas party).
>
> At last this deity seemed to decide that my hulking, looming mass was distracting her from her homework, and she motioned me to an area to the left of her desk, where I obediently stood. Finally, she told me I could sit down. I thought that was very thoughtful

of her, but I couldn't find anything to set my considerable bulk on without courting disaster (by then I had discovered what appeared to be a doll chair next to her desk). But yes, by God, *yes*. The "doll chair" was MY chair. You've all seen those *National Geographic* photographs showing (members of a primitive tribe) squatting with their knees under their chins, staring blankly ahead. You now have the picture of my posture. . . . It was going to be a long fifty minutes.

Stigen makes us laugh at professionals, all right. But she is also uncanny at expressing the unsettling discomfort many parents used to feel in the presence of such trained people.

On the other hand, professionals did not always feel comfortable with parents. And the more prim and perfect those highly trained ones appeared, the more they may have been putting up a false front to hide their own feelings of inadequacy.

I recall a psychologist who was deathly afraid of nonprofessional encounters with the parents of his clients. On one occasion, he left a shopping cart full of groceries in the aisle of a supermarket and quietly walked out when he spied a parent shopping in the same store.

These discomforts extend to other professions, as well. I was once invited to a Hooray-It's-Over-Again party, held by school teachers who were celebrating the end of their semester parent-teacher conferences. Imagine that! After all those years of attending uncomfortable sessions and trying to avoid slips like, "Hello, Ms. Prim, I'm Robert Failure. Tell me where I am a flop as a father this time." After all those years of gosh-I-must-be-a-lousy-parent feelings, suddenly and a little too late, I learned that teachers felt just as incompetent around me! But that was then.

Today, when you observe boys and girls with handicaps performing skills that, a couple of decades ago, none of us thought they could accomplish, take a closer look.

More often than not, you will find parents and professionals working together as teammates, in such ways as . . .

parents in classrooms from time to time
teachers in homes
learning from each other
continuous two-way communication (notes, telephone calls, meetings)
developing individual education plans together
discussing divisions of labor (what tasks in home, classroom, neighborhood—and for how long)
emergency meetings
happy communications (guess-what-Jim-did-today messages)
evaluating progress
sometimes laughing for joy after an achievement
other times, feeling whipped
patting each other on the back
respecting each other
knowing how much they need each other.

What happened to the discomfort? I guess nobody had time for it. Too much attention and energy was being expended on pinpointing a child's specific developmental delay and on determining what each person could do about it. When a this-kid-needs-us-all-so-let's-go-to-work attitude becomes uppermost in everyone's mind, parents and professionals often become close-knit comrades with a common cause. Without their planning it—or even thinking about it—it happens.

When partnerships like these really click, it often carries over into other areas. For example, in Nebraska, from 1967 through 1975, some parents and professionals worked so closely together that they developed a common human-service philosophy and specific goals for achieving it. Then they became active with the governor and state lawmakers in a massive overhauling of legislation for persons with developmental disabilities. They developed state plans, county plans, attitude-change programs, re-gionalized community-based service systems, and funding to operate the programs.

Parents and professionals had come as partners to the state capitol at Lincoln from places like Norfolk, Hastings, Scottsbluff, Ogallala, and Omaha. They had delivered a "double whammy" to state government. Parents spoke in hearings and approached legislators in the foyer. They spoke clearly about the problems people with handicaps faced in Nebraska. And, of course, legislators—being used to such people—knew how to listen respectfully, thank them for coming, and quietly shrug it all off a few minutes later. But no sooner did the parents finish than their sidekicks—the professionals—took over, providing the lawmakers with detailed statistics.

It was obvious to everyone that neither the parents or the professionals alone could have influenced the government so powerfully. It was their well-planned, carefully detailed teamwork that did it. Many senators expressed amazement at the effectiveness of that. Said one, reminiscing at a later date, "You people were too much. If we could have kept you apart, we would have been OK. But when you came at us together . . . well, you were too much."

Later, when professionals in other, larger, more powerful states began to wonder how such a conservative state as Nebraska could have increased the quality of living for persons with mental retardation in such a short time, two of the movement's leaders explained.

We are now convinced that failure of parent and professional to cooperate *truly* and *genuinely*, rather than merely working alongside each other, must have accounted for the failure of many a planning effort, and for some of the confrontational clashes in certain large states. And in our opinion, those professionals who believe that substantial sustained progress can be achieved at the agency level alone, without regard to the consumer or to cultural concurrence, will be doomed to eventual failure in their enterprises.[1]

1. W. Wolfensberger and F. Menolascino, "Reflections on Recent Mental Retardation Developments in Nebraska," *Mental Retardation* (December 1970).

Strong words. They remind us never to underestimate the power that can be developed when parents and professionals pull together to help a child with a handicap.

Consider These Options

- Stop feeling insignificant in the presence of professionals.

- Look for professionals willing to team up with you.

- Know that you and only you possess and can provide crucial information about your child with a handicap.

- Never think you must apologize for asking professionals to join with you in developing training programs for your son or daughter.

- Do not feel you always must be so patient. A biological developmental time clock is ticking away inside your child. He or she is already behind schedule on some things. Do everything you can to see that neither you or a professional wastes your child's time.

The only consumer service that can regulate itself successfully is that of the parachute packers—they must test their own products. Other services cannot renew themselves without feedback from their customers.

In the field of developmental disabilities, good interaction between consumers and hands-on workers definitely is needed, but that is not enough. Leaders who operate above such side-by-side relationships also need clear communication from those who receive the services. After all, agency directors, school principals, and bureau chiefs control the planning, the use of funds, and the delivery of the services which ultimately shape the destinies of persons with handicaps. Therefore, these shapers need shaping, too. Here are some specifics.

Serving persons with handicaps has become big business, and no business can remain efficient unless it hears from those it serves.

Listening to feedback only from those the agency chooses to hear is not enough. Such behavior often leads to the rubber-stamping of agency decisions and plans.

Complaints will improve a service more quickly than commendations.

Salaries of workers in agencies need scrutiny. Service efficiency diminishes when some workers receive high salaries for doing little, while others almost kill themselves for the minimum wage.

Technically, persons with handicaps are the true consumers. Nevertheless, parents and other family members usually are the communicating consumers.

Parents and other family members possess an invaluable perspective. Because they live with the persons who are receiving the services, they are in an excellent position to know those persons's specific needs and whether they are satisfied. No other worker can fully duplicate this perspective.

Bureaucrats and parents do not always agree as to whether a program works well. For example, a writer can interview a program director who—with the use of charts, graphs, and timelines—convinces the journalist that these programs are "the best in the nation." (The number of bureaucrats who believe their programs rank on top is awesome.) But when parents describe the same program, the interviewer gets a completely different story. Somehow, the *rhetoric* delivered by some bureaucrats fails to match the *performance* observed by the parents. Persons with handicaps in mixed-signal programs such as these can suffer irreparable harm.

Thorough program planning must include both service-agency leaders and consumers. Of course, if parents do nothing, insensitive bureaucrats are happy to go along without consumer input. They can build do-nothing programs, place elaborate public relations facades around them, and get paid . . . as long as consumers sit back and let them. Eric Toffler warns that this turn of events in countries such as Canada and the United States now reaches frightening proportions. Such one-sided planning "takes on an elitist character that removes decisions from the ordinary citizen and hands them over to remote experts and bureaucrats" (*The Eco-Spasm Report* [New York: Bantam Books, 1975]). Toffler claims that grassroots people—such as parents—are needed "to help (and watch) the planners."

So you have decided to be a candid consumer, a fearless-feedback-giver-to-the-top when things go wrong with the services delivered to your son or daughter. That sounds simple. You plan to go to bureau chiefs, just as Nathan went to King David and convinced the monarch he was wrong for messing around with Bathsheba and for having her husband put out of the way. (Nathan made it look easy—he forced David to fall to his knees in remorse and blubber a plan of restitution.) Or you decide to go, like strong but kind Marshal Dillon, who calmly placed his hand on his holstered gun and, with no-nonsense timber in his voice, said, "I'm tellin' you, Dirk, you cannot do what yer doin' any longer." (It was a piece of cake when Matt did it. Dirk, being no fool, stopped doin' what he was doin', thanked the marshal for the advice, and shaped up.)

But when you go to the director, principal, or bureau chief with your feedback, he or she may not respond as did David or Dirk. Some bureaucrats possess an uncanny number of responses to give you the impression they think you are an ingrate, a troublemaker, or a weird person. It can set your head spinning. Such leaders preach their own brand of tell-us-where-we-are-wrong-because-we-need-to-know sermon. But when you really tell them, they make you feel as though you were a deviant.

Why? Anthropologist Laura Nader, who recently finished a massive study of consumer-complaint failures throughout North America, gave an interesting explanation in an article titled "Complainer Beware" (*Psychology Today* [December 1979]).

> The imbalance of power gives producers a psychological, as well as an economic advantage over consumers. One and a half centuries ago, de Tocqueville observed that as a people, Americans are intolerant of deviant or eccentric behavior. A prime technique in handling complainers is to *make them feel like deviants* [author's emphasis], to communicate to the complainer that he or she is out of line, or at least that the complainer's experience is aberrant.

Therefore, you need to improve the power balance between yourself and the bureaucrats in order for your pleas on behalf of your son or daughter to be taken seriously. You must build your own little power generators and crank them up when needed.

See power for what it is. Some persons try to put the idea into your head that power is bad, but power need not be bad. It is neutral. It can be used for good or evil. Good power is beautiful to behold. Your son or daughter needs the products of good power.

Trust your own senses. Consider this real situation, a few years ago.

> What do you do when you are the parent of a mentally retarded eight-year-old who lives in an institution? You admitted Jamie because you couldn't keep him at home; and nobody else in town had any better suggestions. And when you visit your son, you try to believe that he is better off in the institution . . . that the ward attendants are more sensitive to Jamie's needs . . . that the quality of professional care is higher. You force yourself to believe this even on the Saturday when you find your son has a large bruise on his right arm and the ward nurse informs you that he has a broken tooth. (Nobody seems to know how it happened). Then you wonder about the boy's "developmental program" they told you about. He's not hyperactive any more, but he's too quiet and unresponsive.
>
> You want to ask all kinds of questions about Jamie's care. In fact you want to ask so many questions of so many people that someone might think you were doing detective work. But nobody else is asking anything. And you don't want to sound like an upsetter or a troublemaker. So you mindlessly nod . . . and you don't say anything at all.[1]

You too will be caught in darned-if-you-do-and-darned-if-you-don't situations such as that one—uncomfortable positions. Even so, practice the refusal to deny what your senses tell you. In time, power can result.

Know that you are not a deviant. Understand that some bureaucrats make you feel that way to weaken you—to get you to "cave in."

1. Perske, "Speaking for One's Own Child," *Listen Please* (Downsview, Ontario: Canadian Association for the Mentally Retarded, 1978).

Get your facts straight. Real facts, simply stated, lined up one after another can be powerful. Without clear, clean facts, you can go off half-cocked and accomplish nothing.

Write out your facts. Do not try to write them as a professional would. Do it "in your own voice." In other words, sound like yourself. Make a simple list of the points you want to make. Then draw simple conclusions from that list. Remember your ABCs—Accuracy, Brevity, and Clarity.

State your facts calmly. Speak without excitement or hysterics. Practice in front of the bathroom mirror. (I do.) When you are sure of yourself, you will feel more calm.

Make your points in letters. Spoken words can be forgotten or denied. Words on a page are harder to ignore. By the way, do everything you can to get your points on a single page. Bureaucrats do not read as much as they would like you to believe. The top page usually receives the most attention.

Send copies to other powers. Bureaucrats pay more attention to your letter when governors, legislators, advocates, newspapers, TV and radio stations, and other agency heads receive copies. Of course, the audience you muster will judge you according to the facts you raise. Fine. That is, if you know what you are talking about.

Organize with others. In a sense, every voluntary organization for persons with handicaps began in order to correct some sort of power imbalance. Think about the power you can achieve from developing the first eight generators. Then think about the power that could be martialed if, say, eight people came together and carried out the tasks in resonance!

Do not feel the organization must be large. Some six-man bomber teams have made greater impact than thousand-member battleship crews. An alert, committed, well-focused organization of eight competent persons may do more for persons with handicaps than an aimless organization of one hundred.

Support one another in the organization. Learn from the Flying Tigers. When their small squadrons of P-40 fighter planes encountered overwhelming opposition, they flew in a tight circle, each plane staying on another's tail. Then when a "bandit" dived on a plane, the comrade behind took out the bandit. Tremendous power can be generated when small groups of people "cover one another's tails," care for one another, root for one another, and protect one another.

Keep your organization morally honest. Unselfish integrity and a proper moral vision are the only qualities that will keep you from becoming a Mafia. Those people are organized, too. In *War and Peace,* Tolstoy suggested repeatedly that organizations are in continual danger of becoming evil. In fact, he believed that evil groups had an easier time. Reinhold Niebuhr explained why this is so in *Moral Man and Immoral Society.* He describes the way persons with high personal morals, when they become members of an association, agency, or bureau, can lie, cheat, steal, and even murder with hardly a twinge of conscience. Nevertheless, consider the challenge of Leo Tolstoy: "If evil men can work together to achieve their evil ends, then good men can organize for their causes, too."

Organize coalitions. Many small organizations can come together to solve a single crucial problem. The Right to Education for All Handicapped Act (U.S. Public Law 94-142) is the product of such coalitions. Remember, however, that coalitions can work only when all members struggle with the same unifying issue.

Utilize existing due-process laws. For example, when a child's evaluation, placement, or individual education plan is not working, the parents have a legal right to utilize a series of steps, taking as many as necessary to correct the situation. The parent can . . .

discuss the situation with the child's teacher

request to see the child's records

discuss the situation with the principal

request the school district to review the evaluation, program, or placement

request the state board to mediate the disagreement

call for an informal hearing from an impartial panel, at which witnesses and legal advocates can appear to help state the case.

Know the law and utilize it to generate power in your favor.

Get a lawyer. Bear in mind that all powerful principals, directors, and bureaucrats have lawyers ready to move at a moment's notice. Why not you? Journalist Lynn Isbell put it this way.

One snowy morning, a young mother of a retarded boy went to visit the principal of the school her son attended.

"Why," she asked, "does my son have to ride the bus for two hours a day? Why is there no library in this school? Why does this school start later and end earlier than all the other schools in the district?"

The principal was shocked at her ingratitude. Didn't she feel lucky that her son could go to school at all? Did she have to ask for *quality* too? "It's the responsibility of the people higher up," he said.

So she went "higher up" and talked to some administrators who said that the problem was that the district couldn't afford anything better and that, anyway, the decisions were made higher up.

This particular mother had an unfortunate and inconvenient dread of heights and was beginning to feel somewhat dizzy. So she decided to get some company for the climb ahead. It seemed like a lawyer would be good company so she called a lawyer who had no fear of heights at all.

It's amazing how much easier it became to solve some of these problems at less dizzying altitudes after the meeting with the people "higher up" during which the lawyer took copious notes.

This is a true story . . . It doesn't have a happy ending yet, but boy, are things looking up for all the kids in that particular district. You, too, can overcome your fear of heights. (Dougan et al., *We Have Been There*)

Go to court. Powerful people—millionaires, bankers, bureaucrats, institution superintendents, corporation heads, school district leaders, public officials, ranking professionals—go to court at the drop of a hat. J. P.

Morgan became famous for ending unsatisfactory negotiations by saying, "I'll get my lawyer, and you get yours, and let us go to court." But when an ordinary citizen or group of citizens decides to sue, the bureaucrats anguish, wail, and cry foul, as did the mayor of Santo Vittorio.

Why? Because courts are the greatest equalizers of power imbalance that an ordinary citizen can have. Without them, minority groups of all kinds would never have a chance for justice. One of the things that makes our country great is that both bankers and bums can have their cases heard before a no-nonsense judge who calmly listens to rational evidence on both sides of a question and then makes an impartial decision. I am a firm believer in the court system of our land. And I believe it will be a bad day if we ever lose our faith in the courts as our fair and final protectors.

And so, gentle parent, ordinary citizen, keep your kind manner. At the same time, however, remember that you can generate an awesome power, a force that can help your son or daughter with a handicap be accepted, helped, and treated as the rest of this continent's citizens are treated. That is *"kind" power*. For only the strong can be truly kind—the others fake it out of fright.

Powerlessness is a horrible state. It is like standing at the bottom of a well and trying to climb out on a trick ladder—everytime one puts a foot on a rung, it slips down. Do not let anyone render you powerless in that way.

A standard statement in a powerful corporation where I once worked was Power Creates Its Own Opportunities. And it certainly does. In thousands of different ways, power can be used to gain more power.

Power is used to move Amtrak's train 61 from Montreal to Washington, or Air Canada's flight 823 from New York to Vancouver. And power can be used to move people, too.

Use the power you generate as honestly and as fairly as you can. You may not feel the need to generate it for your own sake, but you do need to generate it for the sake of your son or daughter with a handicap.

Consider These Options

● When things are cool and no problem exists, ask to read your son or daughter's records. If there are statements in the records you do not understand, ask someone to explain them. You have the right, and the responsibility, to have this information.

● Before they happen, think about what you will do when you get caught in "double binds" (those darned-if-you-do-and-darned-if-you-don't situations). They will happen. So start thinking about how you will be true to your own senses then.

● Conquer the fear that if you speak out on behalf of your son or daughter, you and your child will surely suffer reprisals. More often than not, the opposite happens. Your son or daughter is usually better off because you had the courage to speak.

● If you become successful at generating power on behalf of your son or daughter, do not hide your story under a bushel. Be unabashed about sharing the steps you took with parents who are still standing at the bottom of the well of powerlessness.

ITEM: *Montreal, Quebec*

Your child is retarded?	Votre enfant est déficient ?
So is ours!	Le notre aussi !
Questions . . .	Vos questions,
. . . Yes, we also had many.	Oui, nous les sommes posées.
Yet, we are content.	Pourtant, nous sommes heureux.
Our family flourishes	Notre petite famille s'épanouit
And life goes on,	Et la vie continue,
Just as we planned.	Aussi belle que nous la souhaitions.
WHY NOT YOU?	*POURQUOI PAS VOUS?*
If you think we can help, call us.	Si vous croyez que nous pouvons vous aider, appelez-nous.

(names and telephone numbers)

PILOT PARENTS   PARENTS-SOUTIENS

Nurses or social workers usually deliver this perky invitation, printed in both English and French, to the bedside of new mothers in Montreal hospitals when it is learned that a newborn has a handicap.

Married couples, parents of children with handicaps themselves, have vivid memories of the way hope and joy evaporated in persons around them after their sons and daughters were born. And they refuse to let other families of persons with handicaps be surrounded by the sad faces they experienced. One Pilot Parent explained:

After the doctor informed me that my newborn girl had Down's Syndrome, sad stories seemed to begin coming from everyone. And deep inside, I knew that there had to be some happy stories, too. Well, I had to find them myself. But it is wrong when one must learn such things so late. We want to help mothers and fathers with newborn mentally retarded babies to know early that a handicapped person is just another person in the family . . . and that life in their family can be as good as any other family. . . . So we meet them when they ask for us, and we share with them how life has been for us . . .

and we give them a chance to see it in our faces. (Perske, "The Need for a Happy Face," *Listen Please*)

Parents like these have outfoxed us. If you read any basic text on retardation, cerebral palsy, autism, or other disability, copyrighted between 1930 and 1950, you will find that the author told professionals to expect only trouble from persons with such children. With authority and detail, the texts predicted that these families would become so depressed, so traumatized, so helpless, that the children with handicaps would need to be sent away as soon as possible.

And yet today, some families have developed such emotional muscle, such wit, such determination, such remarkable world-views that they are sometimes even treated by the rest of us as superparents. Of course, that is a foolish exaggeration. When one is seen as a super anything, one sooner or later fails to measure up. Nevertheless, many have developed such strengths from the experience that was expected to weaken them that they have enough energy, love, and ideas left over to share with other families . . . and with ordinary citizens in their neighborhoods, too.

This sharing takes many different shapes. Travel with me across the continent for a peek at a few examples.

ITEM: *Omaha, Nebraska.* In this city the parent of a child with a disability can call a special number for help, and a Pilot Parent, a "veteran" who has faced the same situation, will make contact within twenty-four hours. Mothers and fathers, after successfully working their own children with handicaps into the nest, sign on for one-year tours of duty as "parents on call." While the Montreal Pilot Parents usually work in maternity wards, their Omaha counterparts make most of their contacts in ordinary community settings. In both situations, however, they do not function as formal counselors, therapists, or case managers. Their guiding strength lies in ordinary, people-to-people contacts: sharing experiences over coffee, telephoning to tell about an article in a magazine, stopping in to help a parent through a crisis . . . comparing notes—always comparing notes. In some cases, whole families get together on picnics. When you are fighting desperately to keep yourself pulled together, something solid, stable, and purposeful can come from relaxed chats over a kitchen table with someone who "has been there" and knows what you are going through.

ITEM: *Seattle, Washington.* Two parents of persons with handicaps decided to produce a manual on ways to obtain services for persons with disabilities. Their idea was simple. They would move through the agencies' processes themselves and then write up the steps they had taken. At the end of one month, however, their plan had been crushed. The red tape and the humiliation they had suffered from some bureaucrats forced them to face a painful conclusion: "We found we were caught up in systems never designed for us and they simply didn't work." So they initiated The Troubleshooters, an organization to help families take detailed steps toward obtaining needed services. And when the steps ran into obfuscations, The Troubleshooters pressured the agencies to clean up their act. Today, parents of persons with handicaps, and other committed persons, after receiving sophisticated training, staff telephones in twenty-four offices throughout Washington state. By telephone, they train "parents in crisis" to become good self-advocates, guiding them step by step through bureaucratic mazes. At the same time, they scrutinize the agencies for barriers that stand in the way. Their motto: "God helps those who help themselves. But the system helps those who know the system."

ITEM: *Nashville, Tennessee.* Most people could not imagine having a "developmentally delayed" or "behaviorally disordered" five-year-old who runs through the house destroying everything breakable . . . screams almost incessantly . . . falls to the floor in tantrums . . . hits, bites, and kicks his brothers and sisters. They would not know your feelings when neighbors insinuate that you are "too soft" as a parent. (When dealt with firmly, this child's behavior becomes worse.) Only when you and your child go together every weekday morning to the Regional Intervention Program do you find people who understand and can help. There you are surrounded by parents who have a child like yours. Those parents do the intake work . . . watch you interact with your child through a one-way mirror . . . coach you on ways to turn off the bad behavior and reinforce the good . . . provide technical explanations . . . come to your home to help you "childproof" it . . . give you a "support parent" who will talk to you on the telephone, day or night . . . and when finally the destructive behavior is controlled, they help enroll your child in public school . . . later, other parents monitor your child's progress in the school. Parents of children with handicaps do this for you *at no charge.* You must agree, however, to one obligation: After your child gains control and begins to develop, you will donate a minimum of nine hours per week for six months to help other parents who come to the Regional Intervention Program.

ITEM: *Omaha, Nebraska.* Now back to the Midwest. Brothers and sisters of persons with handicaps joined with other teen-agers to form a series of small core groups operated by the Greater Omaha Youth Association for Retarded Citizens. Half the persons in the groups were teen-agers with handicaps. As each group became organized, they moved through the town doing what normal teen-agers do—eating at hamburger shops, going to shows, going to church together, traveling across the state to meetings, performing volunteer services for people who needed help, rooting at high school basketball games where one of their members was playing. It became obvious to everyone who knew about the core groups that these people liked being together. Nevertheless, this all-for-one-and-one-for-all attitude did not just happen. The teen-agers received intense training in how to understand and advocate for one another. They developed an uncanny ability to utilize something they called "hidden social training." As a result, their sense of justice became so vivid that they often became the conscience of the parent association in that town.

By now, you have some idea about the ways family members can create strength out of a crisis that was expected to weaken them. If page and print allowed, you would receive descriptions of family members of persons with handicaps throughout North America who . . .

> lobby in legislatures
> monitor agency services
> testify at hearings
> participate in human rights seminars
> conduct public-attitude change efforts
> knock on doors in neighborhoods where group residences are proposed
> start citizen advocacy offices (where citizens are trained to represent the interests of those who cannot speak for themselves)
> support self-advocacy organizations (where people with handicaps help one another speak for themselves)
> start innovative training programs when agencies fail
> develop grapevine lists of understanding physicians and dentists
> develop grapevine lists of professionals to stay away from
> write helpful books on developmental disabilities
> give speeches to community organizations and quite often . . . come to one another's aid in crisis times.

I wish I could gather all the professionals who wrote those textbooks about families of persons with handicaps during the 1930s, 40s, and 50s, and travel with them all over the country to take a second look at some of those families now!

Consider These Options

● Since no two families are alike; and since the perfect ideal family can be found only in books; and since every family is a conglomerate of weaknesses and strengths . . . merely try to be the best family you can be—no more and no less.

● Mother and Father, because some of you have developed so well when you were not expected to, *do not*—I repeat—*do not let anyone treat you as a superparent.* Do not let them sculpt a statue of you and place you on a pedestal. Don't let anyone name a building after you. Those honors are usually reserved for the dead, and you still have a heap of living to do before you get through this life.

● Ponder, however, the increased status that parents of persons with handicaps now often receive from their neighbors . . . and keep going.

---

27. Toward a Better World

I think some families like yours have unwittingly opened a door that leads toward a better world. Let me tell you why.

Some years ago, my mind reeled when I learned how the Eugenics Movement of the early 1900s had pressured and politicked for a better America by testing and discarding persons who had developmental disabilities. My head whirled again when it was revealed that a European country had fought viciously in the 1930s and 1940s to create a superrace. And the Holocaust created remains today too overwhelming for the human mind to fully comprehend. These schemes for isolating or killing persons with handicaps as a means to "improve" society left me, and others like me, baffled and sick at heart.

Then when I became a people worker and a people watcher, a few families in Colorado, New Mexico, Kansas, Nebraska, and Connecticut caught my attention. Each family had a child with a handicap, and they hugged, helped, and rooted for that kid just as they did for their other children. For them, no superrace formulas existed. In spite of the fact that almost everyone tried to discourage them, those families laid loving hands on their children . . . they met in homes and organized . . . they even mustered up enough group strength to knock on doors of community agencies and ask for special programs for their children . . . and when the doors slammed in their faces—which was most of the time, in those days—they found a garage, or an empty house, or a church basement, and they started their own programs.

Of course, those families were in the minority then. I can recall many others who were so whipped to the depths by neighborhood whisperings, children's jeerings, pompous professional predictions, and the they-sure-did-something-really-evil guilts people laid on them that the lives of some of them became utter hell.

But this small group of winners-because-of-no-earthly-reason attracted my attention. With wide-eyed amazement, I listened as they told what it is like to have children with handicaps. I watched their family living at close proximity. I became a member of their organizations and observed the many times they laughed and joked. Amazing! There was nothing in the professional textbooks thirty years ago to indicate that these people could be that happy.

Those parents became my best mentors . . . and they still are.

So my mind is filled with haunting thoughts about folks who attempt to "purify" a country or build a superrace, but also with the unforeseen successes of families who have children with handicaps. And after puzzling over this good-news-bad-news mixture for many years, I have come to some conclusions.

● After two attempts in this century to make the world a better place by shoving persons with handicaps out of it, I believe the ones we tried to reject have become valuable pieces in the puzzle that pictures a truly improved civilization.

● The belief that the world gets better only through the *survival of the fittest* is withering and dying. The robust belief that *we all figure in one another's survival* is taking its place.

● The frenzied competition to become "number one"—or even in the "top ten"—turns my stomach. I would like to leave such efforts behind as I left King of the Hill, a game we played as children, in which we struggled for the top by kicking and pushing others down.

● Labeling persons as "above average" or "below average" in intelligence also causes a dissonant clanging in me. The idea that everybody takes the same narrow test; receives a number; is placed somewhere along the same single, monotonous line; and suffers the indignity of being computed by an expert who then draws The Great Dividing Line and announces that 50 percent of us are above normal and 50 percent are below—this is ludicrous. Just think, if all us "subnormals" sweated and bettered ourselves so as to enter the better-than-normal side, the expert simply moves up and draws another dividing line! Fifty percent of us will never make it.

● Since today's new-breed researchers can identify more than one hundred different types of intelligence, intelligence now is a multiple-choice proposition.

● People were meant to complement each other. Where I am strong, you may be weak. At points where you excel, I may be all thumbs. And the ultimate tragedy comes when I reject you because of your handicaps, and you reject me because of mine. Then we live apart . . . and we die apart. We will die without ever really *knowing* each other or experiencing the rich contributions each could have made to the other's life.

● It is the individual differences in people that add creativity and zest to living. Life becomes downright dull when everyone we know looks like we do, thinks like we do, and acts exactly as we do.

● Genuine scientific facts and healthy social change first appear in the world as small hard-to-explain "anomalies" (such as the successful parents of persons with handicaps who came onto the scene recently). Somehow these anomalies cannot be explained away. They grow larger. They cause conflicts between old ways of thinking and the new way that the anomaly represents. They keep coming . . . and

coming . . . until a knowledge breakthrough takes place.

● Breakthroughs-in-the-making appear slowly and painfully. Those who work for them put in long hours, go through anguish, and sometimes when the pressure is almost too much, they say things such as, Why can't others see what we see? Will we ever make it? Will it ever happen? Then the breakthrough happens, and it strikes almost everybody like a bright light. Finally the breakthrough becomes second nature to most folks. They accept it; it is seen as no big deal. But we sometimes look back at the history of the change, and we wonder, Why did it take so long?

● Progress in social change is uneven. There are setbacks. Therefore, believe that it is better to fail in a cause that will ultimately succeed than to succeed in a cause that will someday fail.

● Contemporary, forward-thinking human beings experience not one, but two irresistible strivings. They struggle to achieve their own highest potential. But at the same time, as Bill Cosby once said, "strive to reach back and grab their brothers and sisters, too."

● The most important conclusion of all: *The more advanced a civilization becomes, the more it will understand, value, and relate healthily to its members who have severe handicapping conditions.*

There you have them. These unfinished bits of insight make sense to me because I became interested in families like yours. Stir these ideas around in your own mind. Feel free to ponder them individually—to accept some, reject some, modify them, expand on them, or add some of your own. Have you really opened one more door toward making a better world? I think you have.

PERSKE

This book has ended. These new directions challenge you to take fresh looks in many directions: within yourself; toward your child, your family, your neighborhood; and even into the future.

Of course, these signposts point in idealized directions; merely reading them is easy, but following them can be downright rough. Actually, no family—we repeat—*no family* will move from sign to sign with ease. Every family incurs breakdowns, detours, and setbacks, and so will yours. If you did not, your genuineness as human beings could be questioned.

There are more signposts. Nevertheless, understanding these directions and following them for awhile may prepare you for finding others farther down the road.

By now you may have noticed that the art and words of this book usually mirror the victories and successes we have found in families like yours. Make no mistake, we could have reflected hundreds of grim vignettes showing families being pushed into almost unbearable sloughs of despond. We refused to do that. Of course, we know there is a tough side, too. But we believe that someone needs to hold up directions that point toward the good, the beautiful, and the valuable, rather than dwelling so long and so loudly on the bad and the ugly. Gloomy views often are easier to describe than successful ones. That may be why newspapers and news broadcasts usually emphasize the gloomy side of life . . . and that may be why more people buy newspapers and watch newscasts which, for the most part, portray that side of life. Therefore, forgive us please for failing to function as undertakers, choosing instead to be optimistic direction pointers.

On the other hand, many families such as yours can describe new directions better than we can. Two examples follow.

Some years ago, a young parent of a child with developmental disabilities received understanding and guidance from a member of the Pilot Parents of Omaha. Those peer-group relationships helped her so much that today this woman works as a coordinator within that organization. We asked her to describe new directions for families of persons with developmental disabilities as she saw them. She did, and she put them all on one typewritten page!

We have all experienced the feelings, the guilts, the hurts, the glooms. The feelings are very familiar to us. It is difficult to cast away what is familiar and enter into the unknown, but we must. Experiencing our feelings is healthy. Wallowing in them is not. We are called to move from weird times to the challenging times ahead. The responsibilities that challenge us are:

To Educate Ourselves. To become knowledgeable and articulate in all matters regarding our children. We can only do this by getting the answers to the questions. We must become authorities regarding our children.

To Become Politically Astute. We must know what laws benefiting our children are in existence, what laws are needed, and how we can assist in their passage and implementation. The politicians have to know what we want before they can deliver.

To Educate the Public. To achieve an awareness that our kids are positive, contributing members of society. If we don't tell the community, how will they ever know?

To Become Involved with Other Parents. If there is not a parent support or parent advocacy organization active in your community, start one. Numbers have impact. Only with all parents working toward a common goal can the full effect of P A R E N T P O W E R be realized.

To Express Our Feelings. Our children and their rights are emotional issues. If we don't let our feelings be known, nothing will happen.

To Assert Ourselves. Only when we demand our rights without damaging the rights of others can we be comfortable in the role of one who brings about change.

To Create Living Experiences and Opportunities for Our Kids. Our children don't always have the chance to have a best friend, clean their room, receive personal mail, or go shopping. Sometimes we must make these things happen so our kids can achieve their greatest potential. Think about it.

To Be Willing to Risk. Before any social change can occur, we must be willing to risk on a very personal level. No one else has the same kind of commitment. In other words, stick our necks out.

To Laugh. We must laugh at life and at ourselves. It's called survival.

To Be Gentle with Ourselves. Take a break, go to a movie, chat with a friend, eat a brownie, don't eat a brownie—above all, strive to be happy.

Glenda Davis

Twenty-one years ago, an editorial from a national newspaper was distributed to professionals in an institution where I worked. It was an editorial about Christmas and mental retardation, written by Eric Sandahl, whom none of us knew personally. The fact that Sandahl wrote out his experience as a *parent* of a child with retardation amazed us. As I have pointed out, at that time most professionals viewed parents as traumatized, helpless individuals who only messed things up when they became involved in the care and treatment of their own children. Since then, Eric-of-the-Quiet-Strength has become a valued personal mentor. His editorial provides touching directions even today.

I knew almost nothing about retarded children ten years ago. What I knew made little impression. As a newspaperman you're supposed to have a fair knowledge of disease and defect. . . . In my growing up, in my work, and in the Army, I had been exposed to a certain amount of "life in the raw," but I was really a stranger to human suffering and severe handicap.

Perhaps if the tragedy of mental retardation had never touched my life, everyday experience would have taught me many of the lessons of human understanding which today I inextricably associate with the cause of the retarded.

That may be true, but I don't believe it.

I do not believe that in the ordinary course of events I would have come to appreciate how misfortune can propel "ordinary" people to great heights of performance and leadership; how a single-minded, selfless whole can become far more than the sum of its parts.

. . . Nor would I have learned the sympathy I feel today for all types of handicap and suffering, or my insight into the infinite ways in which natural and social barriers stand in the way of happiness and fulfillment for so many human beings.

. . . Nor would I have so often seen false values and false counselors crumple in the face of human catastrophe, and great courageous souls rise out of them.

. . . Nor would my impatient spirit have learned to find happiness in small things, in the little steps that ultimately lead to great progress.

. . . Nor would I ever have seen such massive evidence of the spark of divinity that burns in every man, if only there is a cause to light it.

. . . Nor would I know the depth of the love of the one who vowed with me, "for better or worse," who suffered the worst, and who is stronger and nobler because of it, to me and to all who know her.

. . . These are the gifts I hold most precious in this Christmas season as my tenth year in the world of the retarded draws to a close. These are the guiding lights that dispel the darkness into which I was cast so abruptly ten years ago.

. . . What greater gifts could I ask?[1]

We hope these new directions will give you and your family some rich targets to shoot for. Keep going!

---

1. *Children Limited* (Arlington, Tex.: Association for Retarded Citizens—National Headquarters, December 1959).